Y0-BUB-596

Beyond Yiddishkeit

SUNY Series in Anthropology and Judaic Studies
Walter P. Zenner, Editor

Beyond Yiddishkeit

*The Struggle for Jewish Identity
in a Reform Synagogue*

FRIDA KERNER FURMAN

State University of New York Press

Published by
State University of New York Press, Albany

©1987   State University of New York

For information, address State University of New York
Press, State University Plaza, Albany, N.Y., 12246

Library of Congress Cataloging in Publication Data

Furman, Frida Kerner, 1948-
    Beyond Yiddishkeit.

    (SUNY series in anthropology and Judaic studies)
    Bibliography: p. 143
    Includes index.
    1. Judaism—United States. 2. Reform Judaism—United States. 3. Jews—United
States—Identity.
I. Title. II. Series.
BM205.F87 1987   2.96.8'346'0973   86-29999
ISBN 0-88706-513-9
ISBN 0-88706-514-7 (pbk.)

To Roy

Contents

Contents

Acknowledgments

I would like to thank the people of Temple Shalom—members, clergy, and staff—for making this study possible. Beyond that, however, I want to thank them for their hospitality, warmth, and generosity. I learned much from Temple Shalom, not only about how a synagogue structures Jewish meaning for its members, but also how its inhabitants give meaning to each other's lives. This is a community of people who genuinely care for each other: They taught me a great deal about the human possibilities of organized religion.

Many individuals generously provided encouragement and suggestions at various stages of this study. I wish to thank Stanley Chyet, David Ellenson, Donald E. Miller, Norman Mirsky, the late Barbara Myerhoff, John B. Orr, Riv-Ellen Prell, and the four anonymous readers designated by the State University of New York Press. I am deeply grateful to Jane Monnig Atkinson for her friendship, unswerving support, and thorough critique of the manuscript in the last stages of revision. I also thank my editor at SUNY Press, Rosalie Robertson, and the series editor, Walter Zenner, for their suggestions. Of course, I take full responsiblity for the interpretations offered herein. Shulamit Levine's skills on the word processor are most appreciated. I gratefully acknowledge the support of the Memorial Foundation for Jewish Culture, which provided me with a grant in the initial stages of this project.

My husband, Roy Furman, was a marvelous counselor, critic, editor, and child-care provider—as the needs arose—throughout the time that this book was in process. The dedication is a small gesture of my appreciation.

Introduction

Concern with personal identity has become a preoccupation in contemporary America. Whereas in the past the question of self-definition was thought to belong to the province of adolescence, today the quest for identity spans the life cycle. This question not only raises philosophical, existential concerns, but it addresses also the perceived displacement of the self from the group: It asks, "Who am I?" but also, "Where do I fit in?," "What is my niche?"

This interest in identity is equally salient in the Jewish community, where concerns with identity include collective, as well as personal, meanings, and the survival of Judaism as such is seen to depend upon the identity of its adherents. Contemporary Jewish identity is a complex phenomenon, one that has been subjected to a variety of influences. Jews left the ghettoes of Western Europe and the *shtetls* (small towns) of Eastern Europe and began their entry into the surrounding societies as recently as the nineteenth century, as late as the early part of the twentieth. Not only were they exposed to very different social milieux in this transition, but they also experienced a clash of consciousness: from traditional to modern culture.

This move from segregation—physical, as well as cultural—to integration into the larger society involved tensions brought about by a rapid confrontation with modernization, a process that had been gradual in its evolution, at least in Western Europe. This experience is reflected in tensions in Jewish identity to this day, tensions between religion and secularism; collectivity and individualism; tradition and modernity; and religious, ethnic, cultural, and nationalistic self-images. The American situation has contributed its own particularities to these tensions.

These tensions have transformed Jewish identity from a generally ready-made, automatically embraced configuration of meanings in premodern times to a complex, fractured, and often painfully and

1

incompletely constructed one in the present day. Given the complicated nature of Jewish identity today, we are forced to ask how Jews "become" and remain Jewish in modern America; that is, what are the processes of Jewish identity construction and identity maintenance? Beyond that, however, we must explore the content of that Jewish identity, namely, what makes that identity Jewish? Finally we must ask, does this identity work?

This book is about American Jewish identity, and these are some of the central questions that it addresses. More specifically, it is an ethnographic study of the life of an American Reform synagogue, Temple Shalom (a fictitious name). Its aim is to examine mechanisms of identity construction at Temple Shalom in the light of modernity and its impact upon contemporary Jewish identity.

In retrospect, the decision to study American Jewish Reform identity reflects two axes in my personal life: my status as a first generation American, and my intrigue with Jewish religious practice in a secularized world. I first became interested in questions regarding identity as a young teenager newly arrived in America. I was born and raised in Chile, and, after a brief sojourn in Argentina, my family made its home in the United States. Language aside, there was a sufficient disparity between my South and North American experiences to make for a fascination with American culture, a fascination that continues to this day. A feature of American society that struck me forcefully, even at a young age, was the high degree of malleability that characterizes Americans' social location. The self seemed much less attached to family, locale, and ethnic or religious groups than its Latin American counterpart. At the same time, I noted with astonishment the enormous pressure towards conformity among my American high school peers, whose preoccupations with school rings, sweaters, and drill team membership were beyond my ken. Thus began my interest in American identity. My outsider's perspective has been softened with time, but its edge has been put to good use in the observations and concerns of my adult life.

Today I am a liberal Jew, involved in Jewish religious and cultural concerns. This has been an evolving perspective, since the Judaism of my childhood was of such a different type. Orthodoxy was the only religious option for Chilean Jews in the 1950's, and most opted for ethnic, cultural, and Zionist alternatives. So did my family. My involvement with Reform Judaism began cautiously during my college years and developed more earnestly during graduate school. I came to appreciate the seriousness of Judaism in the lives of eminently modern individuals and to partake of it.

My training in social ethics, with a strong emphasis on the sociology of religion, directed my attention to questions of religious meaning, value, and identity in modernity. Most social ethicists do not study values on the basis of ethnographic studies. My interest in contemporary Jewish identity was such, however, that I felt that none of the usual approaches to its study—"armchair" reflections, the investigation of exceptional Jews (such as writers, theologians, rabbis), sociological surveys—would do in addressing my concerns as to how "ordinary" Jews in fact construct their Jewish identities.

I thought it crucial to treat an institution instead of unaffiliated individuals as the focus of the study because I believe that identity is forged in the dialectic between individual and collective intentions, not in the solitude of the individual Jew's heart and mind. Values and meanings about "being Jewish" are neither strictly personal nor collective in nature but somewhere in between, formed by the interplay between individual projections and institutional objectifications. An institution thus provides a bounded universe within which to explore definitions about Jewish identity that have evolved, through time, out of this interplay of meanings.

I chose a synagogue as my research setting because, more than any other existing American institution, it addresses the variety of meanings associated with being Jewish. No matter how secularized Jews have become, it is finally impossible to separate the meanings of Judaism, the religion, from Jews, the people. In addressing religious, as well as other, components of Jewish identity, Temple Shalom reveals, not only how community and identity are developed, but also how religious life is constructed. The link between identity and religion is therefore central in this study.

I selected a Reform synagogue from the spectrum of available Jewish religious options in America—Orthodoxy, Conservatism, Reconstructionism, and Reform—because of the Reform movement's consistent commitment to modern life and thought and its radical departures from traditional definitions of Jewish identity. I therefore felt that a Reform synagogue would most pointedly address the dilemmas that modernity has imposed on Jewish identity.

Informed by a social science background and methodology, I nonetheless see this book as a study in social ethics. I have been strongly influenced by the late H. Richard Niebuhr's (1963, 47–68) view that the social ethicist must begin with a descriptive agendum: to discover "what is going on" morally in a community, to "lay bare the roots and fundamental character of a community's moral life" (ibid., 13).[1] The ethical enterprise thus involves the articulation of a community's values, ethos, and identity. One way to think about a community's sense of self—its ethic—is to key in on the ways that is members say "we" (Sellers 1975, 40). Here I explore Temple Shalom's "we-saying," not only by focusing on verbal speech, but also by examining its liturgy and ritual practice, its physical space and aesthetics, its communal life and ideological commitments. This is what much of the book attempts to do.

The prescriptive task, according to Niebuhr, may follow only upon the heels of this kind of descriptive work: "Out of this discourse in the community. . .can come an understanding of what ought to be done" (1963, 13). The book is organized along Niebuhr's scheme. The first two chapters provide a context for locating Temple Shalom historically and ideologically. Chapter Three, Four, and Five describe and analyze Jewish identity at Temple Shalom in three facets of synagogue life, following Wach's (1944, 19–34) typology of religious life: ideology, ritual, and communal expression. The conclusion, Chapter Six, moves from description to prescription. Here I see my task as a social ethicist to be twofold: first—a task begun in previous chapters—to articulate the members' sometimes explicit, sometimes inchoate feelings and conceptions regarding Temple Shalom and its future direction; and second, from this articulation to evaluate the viability of the identity it offers them.

My ethnographic approach was a phenomenological one. In agreement with Alfred Schutz (1971) and other phenomenologists (see, for example, Colaizzi 1978), I believe that a critical task of the social researcher is to begin with the subjects' experiences, that is, with the meanings attached to particular actions and attitudes by subjects from their own frames of reference. I entered the field with a very broad interest in contemporary Jewish identity. In phenomenological style, I attempted to bracket my own preconceptions and assumptions about what goes into the constitution of Jewish identity, so as to allow Temple Shalom and its members to shape my understanding of what was important in their community and not vice versa. A principal concern in both the data-gathering and analytic phases of this study was to describe Temple Shalom members' experience of their own and the institution's Jewish identity.[2]

Entry into Temple Shalom was relatively unproblematic. I initially approached one of the rabbis, with whom I had a prior acquaintance, about the project. Excited about it, he took the proposal to the board of trustees and secured board members' authorization for the study. He subsequently graciously introduced me to the congregation, both to small groups of people at meetings or cultural activities and to the institution as a whole through the Temple's bulletin.

Initially a few members seemed to feel uncomfortable about "being watched" or resentful about "being used as guinea pigs," but the majority seemed very interested in, and supportive of, the project. Besides the rabbi's support of me, two other factors seem to have served as legitimizing agents. The fact that I am Jewish appeared important to a number of people, who, upon meeting me, asked me if I was. I expect that the fact that my husband is a rabbi also served as a legitimator of me and my study, judging by the frequency of reference to it.

A Jewish participant-observer of a community of Jews could conceivably encounter problems: alienation from the site of study or fusion with it (i.e., "going native.") Given my nonreligious upbringing, synagogue life was not second nature to me, so I approached Temple Shalom with an appropriate distance. Yet my acquired knowledge of religious Judaism and my strong Jewish involvement provided access to subtle and sometimes subjective meanings possibly lost on the total outsider (see Heilman's [1980] discussion of the "native-as-stranger" on this point).

The field of study was largely conducted during the course of one year, 1978. I spent the initial five months completely involved, virtually on a daily basis, in every facet of congregational life: worship services, special holiday celebrations, committee and staff meetings, study groups, lectures, social activities, and one weekend retreat. Participant observation was the major research tool during this time, although formal and informal open-ended interviews with the staff were also conducted.[3]

I attended events on a more selective basis for the next seven months. During all phases of participant observation, numerous informal interviews were carried out with congregants, most often during meetings and at the social hour following Sabbath services. In addition, I conducted formal open-ended interviews, involving tape recording and note taking, with both members and clergy during prearranged meetings. I interviewed fifteen members in their homes;

these interviews generally lasted for four hours and were divided into two sessions. Interviews with the clergy were conducted at the Temple; these varied in frequency, duration, and intensity. I conducted
one interview with the religious school principal. Interviews with other
Temple staff were informal in nature. I purposely postponed formal
interviews with members in order to develop rapport and trust. After
seeing me around for five months, members were most cordial and
eager to be interviewed. All acceded to being tape recorded.[4]

As the study proceeded, a tapestry of meanings associated with
Temple Shalom's Jewish identity began to emerge across a variety of
different areas of synagogue life: religious services, holidays, business
meetings, board and committee meetings, social events, social interactions, casual conversations, sermons, structured interviews. The
data collected was extensive but impressively consistent in regard to
the prevailing understanding of Jewish identity at Temple Shalom.
Choices became necessary during the various phases of the study.
In general, I decided to focus on those public meanings available to
the congregation, as a whole, and not the private perspectives of the
clergy. While individual expressions of Jewish identity received attention in data-gathering, the accent was placed on the most active
members. Research was conducted during 1978, so my observations
and conclusions naturally reflect that period of time in the life of Temple Shalom. In the interest of confidentiality, the synagogue's exact
location and precise demographic characteristics are left intentionally
vague. Subjects' voices—including the clergy's—are likewise not
explicitly identified. It is, of course, impossible to cover *all* aspects
of life at Temple Shalom in a single volume. I believe, however, that
the pages that follow provide a clear and representative picture of
Temple Shalom, its ethos, values, and identity.

To what extent does Temple Shalom typify American Jewish
identity, in general? I sense that the crisis in Jewish identity observed
in this study is a widespread phenomenon among contemporary
American Jews. No doubt Jewish identity is negotiated in different
ways by different Jews today. In the absence of comparative studies
of other congregations,[5] it is hard to say to what extent Temple Shalom
is unique in its attempts to solve the dilemmas and travails of identity
construction for its members. On the one hand, it is clear that this
synagogue's central interests are not focused on such matters as
ethnicity, religious observance, the Holocaust, or feminism, the stuff
of other Jews'—and surely other Jewish institutions'—Jewish identity

today. On the other hand, Temple Shalom reveals powerful continuities with dimensions of European and American Jewish life in the twentieth century in its concerns with liberalism and social justice. By providing a dense study of identity in one Jewish institution, this book thus may make a contribution to understanding particular processes involved in identity construction by American Jews. Other studies would surely round out the picture.

ONE

The Transformation
of Jewish Identity

Travelers from a different time and place might have a difficult time, on first blush, recognizing members of Temple Shalom as Jews. This would be the case should their perspectives be those of the Middle Ages, eighteenth-century Europe, or even contemporary Chassidic communities in New York City. They would see people who, though self-admittedly Jewish, nonetheless feel confused and sometimes ambivalent about their Jewish identity. They would note that many join the synagogue to make friends or to send their children to religious school and not principally to pray or to study. They would observe that many members attend religious services only once a year, for the high holidays, while others come occasionally, with only a very small minority attending regularly. They would wonder at the lack of religious observance, seeing that all members ride on the Sabbath, most do not observe dietary restrictions, and few are interested in following many of the commandments required by Halacha (the Jewish legal tradition).

Yet Temple Shalom members are not an aberration when seen in temporal and spatial context. In some respects, they resemble the majority of American Jews today. In other ways, they manifest distinctive tensions in the manner in which they construct their Jewish identity. Jewish identity has never been a static phenomenon; rather, throughout Jewish history it has been molded both by contact with non-Jewish cultures and continuity with the Jewish past. The last two hundred years do signal a particularly dramatic rate of transformation, yet continuity with the traditional past proceeds in a variety of styles and configurations throughout the American Jewish map.

Temple Shalom is a Reform synagogue. As such, the identity of its members is mediated by the force of Jewish tradition, modernity, the American experience, and the Reform movement. We shall explore each of these factors, in turn, to arrive at a beginning point for a discussion of Temple Shalom.[1] We shall see that, whether we look at individual or collective manifestations of Jewish identity, the issues are indeed complex and multidimensional.

Traditional Jewish Society

Traditional Jewish society spans the experience of the Jews from the beginning of the Talmudic era (ca. 200 C.E.) to the age of the European Emancipation (first half of the nineteenth century).[2] Unlike other traditional societies, the Jewish society did not form a single socio-geographical entity: Jews lived in numerous locations, establishing many different communities, since the beginning of the Diaspora. Jews also constituted different kinds of sociological configurations prior to modernization: the ghetto and the *Dorf* (village) in Western Europe, the shtetl in Eastern Europe, the "Jewish quarter" in various cities and towns. Socio-economic diversity was also a reality, for some Jews were merchants and peddlers while others worked in agriculture or crafts.

Despite these variations, traditional Jewish society can be seen as a cultural unit, though necessarily through the construction of an ideal type. Here we shall look at some of its basic characteristics in the period immediately preceding its dissolution in eighteenth- and nineteenth-century Europe.

The Religious Dimension

The Jewish tradition generally refers to the written and the oral law (the Pentateuch and the Talmud, respectively), commentaries, customs, and, more broadly, to the history of the people as handed down through time. Of paramount importance in this traditional heritage is the perceived covenantal relationship established between God and the Jewish people at the revelation at Sinai, a relationship whereby the Jews as a community believed themselves to be singled out as the chosen people. This contractual relationship, established in the Bible and elaborated in the Talmud, details the responsibilities of the Jewish people in the form of 613 mitzvot (commandments). These elements—the covenant with God, the status of chosenness, and the obligations inherent in such status—evolved through time into the world view and life style that typified Jewish society before the onset of modernization.

Religion was the basis of collective sentiments, cognitive assumptions, and personal identity to an impressive degree. The conceptions of God, Torah, and Israel constituted the major pillars of traditional consciousness. God was perceived to stand at the center of life, not as a detached or distant God, but, in effect, as a God who, in covenant with the people Israel, was very much a part of their daily lives. The covenant with God—the fundamental religious principle—found expression in Torah, the Law, and its elaborate system of mitzvot. The rigorous fulfillment of these commandments pervaded all of life by structuring time, space, values, interpersonal relations, and social institutions. Life was organized thus, not due to a commitment to ritualism as such, but because powerful religious impulses informed the performance of commandments.

Everyday activities revolved around the major institutions of the society, all of which were infused with religious meanings: the family, the synagogue, the ritual bath, the Jewish cemetery, the ritual slaughterer, the house of study, the *cheder* (school), and the yeshiva (more advanced school). Shtetls were called not only by their names— but k.k. Radom, k.k. Rowno, k.k. Tarnow; k.k. stood for *kehilla kedosha* (holy community) (Schulman 1974, 18). Hence, the shtetl was viewed fundamentally as a place of sacrality.

The synagogue was a central institution, as males were commanded to pray communally three times daily and religious holidays involved special religious services. Sabbath observance was particularly central. In consciousness and in action, the week was divided into the sacred Sabbath and the workweek. The Sabbath was devoted to prayer, study of Torah, rest, and family togetherness. Violations of Sabbath prescriptions were seen as desecrations.

The family and cheder were principal agents of socialization into the traditional world view, as they punctuated time and space with religious ritual, values, and wisdom. Education—the study of the tradition—was a central value, a value upheld by every member of society, regardless of personal status or background. Study was a mitzva (commandment), and thus scholarship was not seen as an end in itself but as a pathway to God. It is not surprising, therefore, that the rabbinic role was the ideal, for the rabbi was the scholar par excellence of Halacha; his major functions were to interpret the tradition and to adjudicate legal disputes when necessary.

Israel, the third pillar of traditional Judaism, refers to the inescapable unity of the Jewish people through space and time. Collective responsibility was manifested by the norm of *tzedaka* (social justice or charity), a religiously prescribed commandment. This religious obligation was institutionalized in a variety of ways and was rewarded by conferring prestige upon the benefactor.

The Individual and the Group

Premodern societies are considered to be status societies, inasmuch as people see themselves and are seen as representatives of groups rather than autonomous individuals. In these societies the social group has priority over the individual, since the individual qua individual has no social standing in society. Society is viewed, therefore, as an organization of social units rather than as an aggregation of individuals (Parsons 1977, 28; Redfield 1947, 302–3).

In traditional Jewish society, Jews were unable to view their humanity apart from their Jewishness. Jewish persons were, irreducibly, Jews, and that gave them their uniqueness in the world.

The relationship between the individual and the community in traditional Jewish society can be illustrated in the operation of the *kehilla* (community). The kehilla was the usual organ of self-government serving the communal needs of Jews in their segregated and often isolated locales. The kehilla normally bound together all Jews who were permanent residents of a local area. The actual association was implemented on the basis of Jewish law, legitimizing its authority through the attachment that community members had to a common Jewish tradition.

The kehilla served a variety of purposes. It was principally a link between the Jewish community and the non-Jewish authorities; hence, it collected taxes and fines for the secular government. It was also responsible for juridical issues, residency permits, administering synagogue and school affairs, and so forth. In other words, the kehilla served as the principal agent of social control. Its greatest tool was the threat of excommunication, the most severe measure of social control available to that society. Since Judaism was a comprehensive way of life, it was far broader than a religious system alone; it encompassed social, ethnic, cultural, national, as well as religious, meanings. Hence, personal identity was constructed and maintained within a *Jewish* frame of reference, and the individual's isolation from that society threatened the collapse of personal identity as a whole. A comparable threat to personal identity issued from the kehilla's power to turn a criminal over to the non-Jewish authorities. This action represented the extreme instance of abandonment of social support, given the Jew's total dependence—material, social, and psychological—on the Jewish community. Of less severity were temporary exclusions from public prayer or the deprivation of some honor in religious leadership. The margin of individual deviation from traditional norms was limited, indeed, given the potential dangers at stake.

This brief portrait of individual-collective relations reveals the traditional Jewish society as a *Gemeinschaft* type of social organization. Tönnies's (1963) celebrated concept refers to a community of persons whose coherence results from a complex of shared feelings, habits, and traditions. Beyond this, however, *Gemeinschaft*-type societies involve mechanisms of "sacrifice, renunciation, and de-individuation" (Bernard 1973, 102), characteristics that point to the subordination of the individual to group goals and norms.

The Power of the Past

In traditional Western societies, the social order is legitimized through the use of the tradition, which is temporally located in the past. Tradition is a concept that is formal in nature and therefore may be associated with any content. Regardless of the content, however, the principal factor that gives power to a specific tradition is its grounding in the past.

The past has been a most significant ingredient in the Jewish traditional mentality. Various reasons account for this temporal emphasis. In the first place, traditional wisdom was rooted in a written document, the Bible, which emerged in the ancient past. Secondly, the precarious nature of life in the Diaspora, its sense of helplessness and state of victimization, led to a stress on "inner" as opposed to "outer" folk memory. Jewish "ethnohistory"—as Patai (1977, 28) calls popular recollection—thus placed a far larger emphasis on internal, religious, and spiritual evolution than on external political, social, economic, or military events through time. Religion reinforced the desire to look inward and backward to the past, to the days of the Temple in Jerusalem and to the words set down through the centuries by the rabbis of old (Brown 1972, 39; see Yerushalmi 1982).

Hence, traditional Jewish society was based on knowledge and values of the past; the future was important only as the hope for the restoration of past values or as a repository of messianic redemption.

The past served as the best guide for the present and future; indeed, decisions large and small were reached by reference to the Halacha, the Talmudic legal tradition.

The Move to Modernity[3]

For the societies of Western Europe, the process of modernization was primarily an internal one, taking place gradually over several centuries. A highly complex process, modernization was responsible for profound social and ideological transformations and changes in mentality. Jewish society remained traditional during the period of Western modernization because of its isolation—externally enforced and self-imposed—from the general cultures in which Jews lived. The collapse of that Jewish society is associated, in large measure, with external factors that penetrated and disrupted its stable characteristics.[4]

The Dissolution of Traditional Jewish Society

The emergence of the Haskala in the second half of the eighteenth century in Germany constituted a major external threat to traditional Jewish society. The Haskala was, in essence, the Jewish counterpart of the Western Enlightenment. Enlightened Jews, known as *maskilim*, made their way into Christian intellectual circles, thereby opening a new avenue of contact with the non-Jewish world.

Many of the early maskilim were people living in two worlds: the world of traditional Jewish thought and practice, on the one hand, and the increasingly secularized, rationalistic, universalistic world of Western Europe, on the other. Maskilim campaigned for the legal integration of the Jews into the larger society, for civil rights, and for the protection of the Jews. Moses Mendelssohn (1729–1786), perhaps the foremost luminary of the Haskala, translated the Pentateuch into German, using Hebrew script, in order to educate the Jewish masses into the German language, thereby facilitating their entry into the larger culture. In order to legitimize the religious life of the Jewish people, he developed a philosophy of Judaism which combined both his particularistic and universalistic convictions. Mendelssohn (1969) essentially conceived of Judaism as a natural religion, whose tenets are accessible through reason, while he affirmed the Jewish ceremonial law as binding.

This and other definitions of Judaism proposed by the maskilim in effect broke with the authority of the Halacha, whether in part or as a whole. The competition of new ideas with the traditional understandings also led to the collapse of the monopoly of the Jewish world view in the consciousness of the people. The increased social and intellectual exchange with the non-Jewish world challenged, as well, the sociological basis of Jewish identity.

As we saw earlier, until this point the sources of personal identity for the Jew had been grounded in a physically and conceptually circumscribed Jewish world. With the opening up of this world, this situation changed. In a letter to Herder, for example, Mendelssohn writes, "Moses, the human being (*Mensch*), is writing to Herder, the human being, and not the Jew to the Christian preacher" (cited in Katz 1962, 170). In conformity with Enlightenment ideology, Mendelssohn saw Jewishness as an aspect—perhaps a compartment—of personal identity and certainly not as its most important component. The universality of humanity had gained center stage.

The Haskala arose in Germany and quickly spread into other Western European Jewish communities; its impact on Eastern Europe was more gradual. Besides a commitment to rationalism and to modern philosophy, the Haskala was also a frequent carrier of secularism. In their desire to become full members of a so-called neutral society—one based on achievement rather than on status ascription—the maskilim campaigned hard to expose traditional Jews to secular studies. Their efforts were assisted, at least in part, by edicts issued in certain parts of Eastern Europe in the first half of the nineteenth century requiring Jewish students to attend state schools.

Additionally, Polish rulers abrogated the power of the *kehillot* (communities), thereby depriving the Jewish society, at least in principle, of its previous social structure. In Russia, the military draft was extended to the Jews, with military service beginning in childhood and continuing for twenty-five years. Family life was thus disrupted, and children were socialized into foreign ways. These developments tended to weaken the communal hold over the individual, a situation that was to become more acute as time passed.

The event of greatest consequence for traditional Jewish society, however, was the Emancipation, which, in effect, gave Jews civil rights and legal equality with other citizens in various nations. The French Revolution was its precipitating event, with the Declaration of the Rights of Man and the Citizen providing a framework for the Jewish Emancipation in France in 1791. Holland followed suit in 1797, Prussia in 1812. Civil rights were given to Jews, though frequently retracted due to reactionary movements, until emancipated status was achieved for Western European Jews by the end of the nineteenth century. In some areas of Eastern Europe emancipation was not attained until World War I.

In time, Jewish identity in Western Europe increasingly became defined by reference to Judaism as a religion, since religion served as the differentiating characteristic in the ethnically homogeneous population of that area. In Eastern Europe, by contrast, Jews came to see themselves as a culture and a nationality, since national-ethnic divisions were the rule there; religion was intimately tied to nationality.

In this manner, the concept of Jewish identity was redefined. It was no longer equivalent to self-identity, as had been the case in the past, when Jewishness embraced religious, ethnic, cultural, and nationalistic meanings. Now, one or another of these meanings became accented or isolated in structuring the Jew's Jewish identity.

Alternative Jewish Paths

Following Emancipation in Western Europe, Jewish aspirations for full participation in society were blocked by deeply set anti-Semitic prejudice. The ticket for acceptance frequently became conversion to Christianity. In fact, many converted, choosing to assimilate completely into the larger culture. Others, desiring to maintain their Jewish identity but wishing to blend more easily into the non-Jewish world, called for reform within the tradition in order to conform more readily to the modern world.

A differentiation of Jewish religious ideology and institutions emerged with the rise of the Reform movement in Germany in the early part of the nineteenth century. Early calls for change—vociferously resisted by traditionalists—were concerned primarily with ritual reform. This was basically an attempt to Westernize worship by introducing a German sermon, choral singing, and the accompaniment of an organ. A Reform ideological position was not developed for some time. Its philosophical underpinnings emerged under the influence of *Wissenschaft des Judentums* (the scientific study of Judaism), a movement largely motivated by reformist impulses.

Once the tradition was submitted to scientific scrutiny, it ceased to function as an authentic and sacred system for those responsive to the new style of investigation. Evaluated by external criteria, the tradition could no longer be as intellectually valid and binding as it had been in the past. Of course, one may assume that by this time the tradition had lost its authority for many Jews anyway. The scientific analysis of the tradition may simply have reinforced the alienation already felt by some.

The reformers, who were the intellectual descendants of the Haskala, wished to enter the social and intellectual arena of the world at large. But another central, motivating factor in the rise of their movement was the reformers' conviction that unless Judaism made peace with the modern world—its demands and its mentality—its future was doomed.

Reform was met by two principal responses: Neo-Orthodoxy, later to become modern Orthodoxy, and Positive-historical Judaism, later known as the Conservative movement. All three were native to Germany and later found expression in America, where they have developed their ideological and practical positions most fully. All three represent varying positions regarding the relationship between the tradition and Judaism in the modern world. Except for the Orthodox viewpoint, the other movements define their ideological perspectives by finding compromises, in varying degrees, between traditional commitments and modern conceptions. (See Chapter Two for a fuller discussion of the American Reform movement.)

As has been suggested, the pattern of modernization for Eastern European Jews was different, with Jewish Emancipation not completed until World War I. While the Haskala made inroads into traditional Jewish society there, the religious tradition remained unreformed. Segments of traditional society became disrupted, however, by the influx of Western scientific, technological, and philosophical developments and by increased urbanization and proletarianization. By the second half of the nineteenth century, when nationalism was the prevailing ideology of the Hapsburg Empire, secular, nationalistic Jewish movements arose in response. Jewish socialists and Zionists had in common their attack on traditional Jewish society (Dawidowicz 1967, 49–63).

With the disintegration of the traditional society, the religious world view of traditional Judaism lost its holistic hold over consciousness, sometimes gradually, sometimes dramatically. This collapse meant a weakening of the collective conscience, to use Durkheim's (1964) term, and of communal control over the individual. In fairness, it must be recognized that many Jews—particularly those who remained involved in traditional Judaism—did not break their collective bonds so rapidly. Indeed, there are Orthodox Jewish communities today which live in self-isolated style and which still adhere to the traditional world view and life pattern. But most Jews, upon entering modernity, experienced many of the same patterns typical of modernization everywhere: individuation, privatization, and secularization.[5]

The authenticity of the traditional religious world view was weakened in the face of competing systems of meaning. The traditional Jewish emphasis on the past as a locus of meaning and value also shifted as Jews became modern. God, Torah, and Israel, once the central tenets of Jewish life and tradition, "have long since parted company from one another and have gone their separate ways: Torah is now scholastic text-study, Israel a foreign State, and God—who knows?" (Neusner 1970, 129). Observance of the commandments— the behavioral counterpart of the Jewish *Weltanschauung* (world view)—likewise waned with the onset of modernization. Among the ceremonial practices, dietary restrictions and traditional dress became impediments to social intercourse or objects of ridicule.

Indeed, the entrance into modern society involved a confrontation of aesthetic modes, as well as ideological clashes or political battles. The shifts to modernity required the Jews to engage in a new social aesthetic, one typical of Western modernity, namely, civility (Cuddihy 1974). To gain acceptance, according to this view, Jews had to modify their social comportment to fit with the civil style of the majority. This involved a change in dress, eating habits, manners, and the embrace of "affective neutrality" (Parsons 1952, 60), the modern tendency to neutralize expressions of emotion in public.

The shift from the Jewish communal basis of organization to the individualism of Western society also had critical consequences for Jewish identity. In traditional society, the individual was born into a secure identity structured by social and religious definitions. By contrast, the modern person increasingly belongs to multiple voluntary associations, has universalistic commitments, and enjoys a status established through achievement. Given these circumstances, it might be said that modern individuals, in large measure, create themselves (Berger et al. 1974, 69–82; Lifton 1970, 37–63).

The major issue emerging from the complex Jewish journey into modernity was a crisis in Jewish identity, one that raised the question of how the Jew can remain loyal to the uniqueness of the Jewish heritage while adapting to the pluralism and secularism of the modern world. Responses to this crisis have been varied, but few would argue with Blau, who maintains that "it is one characteristic of modern Judaism in all its varieties that constancy to the ancestral faith has been more of a problem than has adaptation to the surrounding world" (1966, 27).

With the destruction of European Jewry by the Nazis during World War II, questions regarding the nature of Judaism and Jewish identity in modernity shift to America, the current home of the largest Jewish population in the world. It is in America that the question of Jewish survival in an open society reaches its most critical level.

The American Experience

Jewish adaptation to American society involved conformity to specifically American social and ideological patterns, as well as a continuation of the process of modernization.[6] Jews arrived in America in various stages. The first Jews, Sephardim escaping persecution in Brazil, landed in New Amsterdam in 1654. These and others, Sephardim and Ashkenazim alike,[7] arrived as individuals or in very small groups; they were not part of a mass migration. For more than a century, the synagogue was the seat of authority in the American Jewish community, retaining some disciplinary power over its members.

This situation was to change, however, with the start of the German migrations, beginning in 1836 and continuing for the next four decades. The first waves of German migrants were traditional in religious orientation. The exigencies of their peddling life in American, however, forced the transformation of their lives as Jews, as they found it impossible to maintain religious observance in dietary matters, during the Sabbath, and in other contexts. Acculturation into America and the desire for upward mobility led to further breaks with the tradition. Eventually, Reform ideology and practice, brought to America by German rabbis, was used to give legitimation to adaptations to America already in effect (Jick 1976). Synagogues increasingly became patterned after the Protestant model, with sermon, choir, and organ used to beautify the service. By 1880, most synagogues were identified with Reform Judaism. Concomitantly, Judaism became identified principally as a religion.

The German Jews had moved from immigrant status into the

middle class by the time of the Eastern European Jewish migrations, which started in 1881 and continued until 1924. The new immigrants—the "greenhorns," as they were known to the German Jews—settled in large numbers on the Lower East Side of New York City. An exceedingly arduous life and the new social conditions led even the traditional Jews among them to slacken their religious observance and life style. Adaptation to America for this group had the same consequences as those experienced by their German counterparts. In *The Rise of David Levinsky*, for example, Cahan's hero, who had been a traditional Jew in Russia, declares:

> If you are a Jew of the type to which I belonged when I came to New York and you attempt to bend your religion to the spirit of your new surroundings, it breaks. It falls to pieces. The very clothes I wore and the very food I ate had a fatal effect on my religious habits. (1960, 110)

While the Orthodox synagogue was the rule in the Lower East Side, religious authority—already in crisis when confronted by modernizing impulses in Europe—suffered further losses in America. Here, synagogue organization came to follow the American congregational pattern, each synagogue governed by its own board of lay persons, with the rabbi under its control.

The Jewish immigrant generation succeeded in educating its children and facilitating their exit from the Lower East Side and similar working-class areas. In short order, Jews left their "first settlement" tenements and moved to middle-class neighborhoods. The third generation found itself in the suburbs (Glazer 1972, 79–84).

The immigrants' children, the second generation, became highly secularized. They basically rejected the parents' religion, as their counterparts in other immigrant groups rejected their ethnicity, in an effort to assimilate more fully into American culture. What is significant about this development is that this generation remained Jewish, though its Jewishness had little to do with the Jewish religion. The requirements of the religious traditon, such as the study of Torah, dietary and Sabbath observance, and the laws of ritual purity were largely abandoned. The attachment to the synagogue became a broadly cultural, rather than a specifically religious, commitment (Liebman 1973, 55–56).

In Jewish history, Judaism (the Jewish religion) and the Jews (the

Jewish people) have been inseparable realities. At the very heart of Judaism was the concept of peoplehood. Likewise, Jewish identity was inconceivable without the religious component. The American situation, with some European antecedents, gave rise to a dichotomy between the religious and the national ethnic. American Jewish identity, in large measure, has been constructed through a shifting movement between these polar conceptions (Glazer 1972, 1–8).

Neither Reform Judaism nor Orthodoxy could adequately respond to a Jewishness that was not principally religious in nature. The Conservative movement, which had been founded in the 1880s, appealed to the ethno-cultural inclinations of the large Jewish population constituting the second generation. Conservatism thus became the most popular movement in American Judaism during this time. It proved to be a mechanism for Americanization and social mobility, as well as a form of religio-ethnic identification.

Following World War II, Jewish identity switched from the nonreligious, more ethnic base of the second generation to the religious pole. A marked increase in religious affiliation occurred as a move into middle-class respectability was gained. As Jews moved to the suburbs, their churchgoing Protestant neighbors caused them to question the nature of their Jewish identity and to become self-conscious about their religion. Jews joined synagogues, built buildings, constructed Sunday schools (Glazer 1972, 106–28).

The Nazi Holocaust was another major cause for the third generation's return to Judaism. It gave rise to a reconsideration of the meaning of Jewish peoplehood, and such a concern was sociologically expressed through synagogue affiliation and organizational membership.

Despite the return to religious affiliation, there is ample evidence that American Jews today, by and large, do not follow the religious precepts of traditional Judaism (see, for example, Sklare and Greenblum 1967).[8] Most Orthodox Jews are not strictly observant. The Conservative movement in various ways has accommodated to the demands of modern life by lifting some of the ritual commandments. Reform Judaism has been selective in its subscription to traditional religious demands from the start. Reconstructionism has vastly reinterpreted traditional religious conceptions. Commitments to religious belief and synagogue attendance are generally low among American Jews, though naturally higher among the Orthodox. In addition, while most Jews are highly accomplished in educational achievements, they are generally unlearned in Judaism.

The meaning of Jewish identity, given the weakening of the religious component, is a major issue in American Jewish life today. The concept of Jewish identity varies greatly, but a major question remains as to whether Judaism can survive in freedom. In other words, how can a particularistic group survive in a pluralistic, open society, especially when for most members of that group the commitment to its religious foundations is disappearing? In America, Jewish identity has involved a tension between equally attractive alternatives: integration into American culture and survival as a distinctive group. It is a tension also expressed by the dichotomy between universalism and particularism (Liebman 1973).

American religion has been characterized as moralistic in orientation, whereby religious life has been equated with doing good deeds. This is not a foreign conception in the Jewish tradition. Nonetheless, moralism has been embraced by many American Jews as the sole criterion of Jewish religious behavior, irrespective of religious observance or other Judaic content (Blau 1976, 18-19). Sklare and Greenblum, for example, cite a respondent in their Lakeville study who was reared by Orthodox parents. Although she has departed sharply from the religious orientation of her childhood and retains very few traditional observances, she declares:

> My concept of being a good Jew is being a good person. I wouldn't do anything to hurt anyone. Just being religious [i.e., observant] doesn't make one a good person. Showing a non-Jew what a good person can be without ceremonials is what I believe. I have a belief in the Ten Commandments part of religion and live it without joining the functional part. (Sklare and Greenblum 1967, 94)

Perhaps the most uniquely American trait in American Judaism has been the commitment to what Blau (1976, 19-20) calls "voluntaryism," the conviction that the rights of the individual always take precedence over the rights of society. The individual, rather than the tradition or heritage, is the basis of association in America. Hence all association, including religious organization, is voluntary. The American—and, by extension, the American Jew—experiences not only freedom *of* religion, but freedom *from* religion, as well. The Jew in America finally has gained total freedom from communal control. This development has signalled a radical break with the traditional relationship between the Jewish individual and the community.

Given the Jewish experience in America, it may be suggested that

America has offered the Jews the greatest possibility for safety and prosperity that they have encountered in a non-Jewish land. The openness of American society has also proved to be the most difficult dilemma for Jewish continuity, since the very ease of assimilation threatens Jewish survival. The nature and quality of Jewish survival is another major issue confronting American Jewish life today. As modern people, Jews have broken with the "sacred canopy" (Berger 1969) of their ancestors, thereby breaking with the very tradition that gave meaning to Jewish identity. The content of American Jewish identity is consequently complex and variable. The sources of Jewish community are equally complex, no longer automatic in the face of individual freedom from group control. The fate of the Jewish people, no longer sealed in the distant past, thus rests in the lives, actions, and volition of individual Jews and their voluntary associations.

Tradition and Modernity
A False Dichotomy

The foregoing discussion depicts the journey from traditional Jewish life to the complexities and vagaries of contemporary Jewish identity in America. This journey reveals a pattern of ongoing adaptations to new times and places, as well as a complex continuity with the tradition. The pattern of transformation and continuity is found in Jewish history in its entirety. What is new in the last two centuries is the *degree* of transformation and consequent disruption to continuity.

Until recently, students of social change tended to dichotomize tradition and modernity and to assume that modernization invariably leads to the truncation of the past. This strict polarization of the traditional and the modern increasingly has come under attack (see, for example, Eisenstadt 1973; Gusfield 1967; Huntington 1971; Rudolph and Rudolph 1967). Instead of presuming that tradition and modernity are dichotomously related in a static way, critics now argue that both are part of a dynamic and dialectical process.

Such new approaches to social change are being applied to the study of so-called modernizing nations, countries currently undergoing rapid industrialization. But there is reason to apply these new insights to the Jewish case, as well. In the first place, the Jewish entry into modernity began less than two hundred years ago, with enclaves of almost completely traditional Jews still remaining today. Second, in spite of the rather drastic changes in identity and consciousness experienced by Jews in their transition to modernity, significant links to the past, whether actual or fabricated, remain. (See Dolgin 1977 and Rotenstreich 1972 for valuable studies of selective use of the tradition by modern Jews.)

Milton Steinberg (1947) suggests that the quest for modern Jewish identity has evolved two types of Jews. Those who refuse to deviate in the slightest from the faith, morality, and practices of their ancestors he calls "strict traditionalists." He contends, however, that those who adapted Judaism to modern ideas and circumstances are also traditionalists:

> The faith they cherish, the principles they pursue, the rituals they observe, the synagogues they frequent—all derive from historic Judaism and are permeated with its values. But they have departed, whether much or little, consciously or inadvertently, from the old patterns. (1947, 10)

Steinberg describes these types of Jews as "modernist-traditionalists." Only because he finds that phrase cumbersome does he call them "modernists," "understanding all along that they are traditionalists, also" (ibid.).

This book explores the construction of Jewish identity in a contemporary synagogue, Temple Shalom, whose congregants and clergy, like the aforementioned students of social change, are strongly inclined to dichotomize between tradition and modernity. Members of this community display a pervasive identification with the modern, frequently contrasting that perspective to their view of Jewish tradition. Prevalent among them is the sense that modernity eclipses the past, that traditional Jewish ideas, practices, and styles are inappropriate for fully modern Jews.

Yet the tradition *in fact* is not so readily dismissed, even by some of the most modern members of Temple Shalom. Because their identity as Jews is linked to a tradition rooted in the past, the construction of that identity must attempt to reconcile a powerfully modern attitude with that Jewish heritage. In this process, elements from the Jewish tradition are selectively addressed or ignored, lauded or denigrated, as this community of modern Jews shapes its identity through a frequently difficult dialogue between past and present. The relationship between modernity and tradition, never an unproblematic one at Temple Shalom, thus emerges as a dialectical process, since in significant ways—to use Steinberg's insight—these "modernist" Jews are also "traditionalists."

TWO

Temple Shalom
Setting and Reform Context

While driving from the valley to the sea, the driver can easily spot a building hugging the land adjacent to the freeway. Temple Shalom is shaped to resemble the ancient Hebrews' tent of meeting in the Sinai wilderness. It is an impressive yet simple, stark concrete structure surrounded by neatly maintained shrubbery and a lush green hillside. A peaceful setting, it is not unusual on occasion to see deer gingerly descending from the hills.

Temple Shalom has not always been located in this serene setting in an affluent section of a large metropolitan city on the American west coast. It was founded by the Union of American Hebrew Congregations in 1947 in order to meet the needs of Reform Jewish residents not sufficiently served by existing synagogues. For the next two years, the small synagogue was housed in makeshift quarters, meeting for services in an old house or a private garden, depending on weather conditions. A major Reform synagogue in the area assisted Temple Shalom in a variety of ways, including the loan of folding chairs and a lectern. It also helped to start the religious school by purchasing school equipment.

Within a year, about twenty families had joined the new congregation. Some members were from the local area; others had recently arrived from the East or the Midwest. A year later, the young congregation recruited its first rabbi, the man who today is its senior rabbi. Under his leadership, a permanent home was found, first in quarters rented from a church, and then in their own building, where the congregation resided until 1963. Membership grew to three hundred families, making for cramped quarters. Given the space limitations, the religious school and the high holiday services could not be conducted in the synagogue. In 1956, land was purchased in the present location of the synagogue, and the move to the new building took place in 1963.

Temple Shalom Today

Members are generally dispersed throughout the area and reach the Temple by automobile, as it is situated in an area without immediately adjacent residential housing. In addition to the synagogue building itself, the land holds a separate set of school buildings a short walk from the main building. An outdoor chapel, located near the school and consisting of a wooden platform and pews made from old railroad ties, is used for small weddings, special services, and religious school programs.

The Presidential Grove of olive trees, situated between the Temple and the religious school, serves as a tribute to past presidents of Temple Shalom. A tree is planted in the president's honor upon completion of a term of office. Together the buildings, the outdoor chapel, the olive grove, and the surrounding greenery constitute a lovely, serene, and well-manicured area.

The sanctuary dominates the Temple's interior (see Chapter Four for a more detailed description). A spacious social hall, separated from the sanctuary by a long folding door, is used for a variety of events, including luncheons and Oneg Shabbat receptions.[1] A library and several small meeting rooms complement the space used by the congregation. The rest of the building contains office space for professional and support staff.

The main entrance of the Temple leads into a spacious, airy lobby. Here the visitor is greeted by the generally aesthetic gestalt that prevails in the Temple as a whole: art on the walls; a sign penned in delicate calligraphy, perched on a simple stand, announcing upcoming events; and a small glass-enclosed display case artfully featuring books or artifacts. Hallways feature walls with original art. The entire building is always neat, clean, and aesthetically arranged. Bulletin boards featuring announcements, common at many synagogues, are absent here.

The Membership

At the time of the study, the membership of Temple Shalom was 550 families, with a membership limit set at 600 families. In general, the members are American-born, affluent, highly educated, and persons or single-parent families belong, but couples or nuclear families are the rule. People of all ages are members, but most active adults range between their thirties and their fifties. Very few elderly people are seen. Some members leave Temple Shalom when their children complete religious school—as is frequently the case in American synagogues—but the majority seem to remain affiliated after this time.

Membership requires payment of dues. These are calculated on an annual "fair share" contribution of 1.5 percent of gross family income. In addition, members are expected to contribute a one-time commitment of 5 percent of gross family income for maintenance and improvement of the Temple building and grounds. Both sources of revenue are based on an honor system, in that it is up to the members to declare their annual income.

Members are somewhat heterogeneous in Jewish background. Many were raised in the Reform movement, but considerable numbers, as well, came from Conservative, Orthodox, or no Jewish background. In contrast to their secular educations, members are largely uneducated in Jewish matters. The vast majority does not engage in daily Jewish practice. Nonetheless, an active minority is very intensely involved in the life of the congregation.

Professional Staff

The professional staff consists of two rabbis, a cantor, an executive director, and a religious school principal. As mentioned, the senior rabbi began his service at Temple Shalom in 1949. Under his direction, the congregation has developed and changed. It is generally agreed that this rabbi has been fundamental in shaping the character of Temple Shalom, from its religious to its aesthetic characteristics, from its philosophical stances to its interpersonal dynamics. The associate rabbi has been with the synagogue since 1972, while three assistant rabbis served the congregation for a period of two years each prior to 1972.

The cantor joined Temple Shalom in 1954, and the executive director came in 1962.[2] Clearly, the professional staff has had a very long, stable involvement with the Temple, a feature that makes Temple Shalom rather unusual among American synagogues.

Organizational Structure

As in American synagogues generally, the congregation itself is the governing body of Temple Shalom. An elected board of trustees, twenty-four in number, serves as the governing agent of the congregation. The board and its committees, in effect, conduct the affairs of the Temple. The committees range from those responsible for the actual maintenance of the institution, in charge of budget and finance, fund raising, and landscape, to those involved with substantive programmatic concerns, responsible for education, the religious school, ritual, and social action. Service committees include the hospitality, membership, personnel, library, and insurance committees.

Members of the board of trustees are elected for a period of three years. Officers are elected for a term of two years by the general membership. The board—including the officers—and the committees are enthusiastic and very active. The governance of the synagogue is typified by cooperation rather than divisiveness. The rabbis are ex officio members of the board, yet they exert far more authority than that status would suggest. The power they are accorded inheres, to an extent, in the charisma of office, a legacy of the authority attached to rabbis in traditional society. The senior rabbi's authority, however, is based, as well, on personal charisma. He is perceived by many congregants to be somewhat removed from the realm of ordinary human beings: He is considered "truly extraordinary," "a superior human being," "an exceptional man." Hence, most decisions regarding the running of the Temple are submitted to him for his reaction. Far from involving only questions of religious import, the senior rabbi is consulted, as well, in regard to fund-raising ideas, aesthetic considerations, and monetary concerns.

The Religious School

The goal of the religious school is to provide children with a Jewish education "in an environment of creativity and joy." The school meets Sunday mornings, except during summertime and holidays. It begins with the first grade and continues through confirmation, which usually takes place at the age of sixteen. Small fees are charged for each student, but Temple dues finance most of the school costs. The Hebrew school, which meets twice a week, prepares children for their bar or bat mitzva, their entry into full religious responsibility and the special service that celebrates it. A religious school principal, responsible to the associate rabbi and to the religious school committee, is in charge of the operation of the religious school.

The Reform Movement in America

Temple Shalom is a Reform synagogue, and its Reform affiliation is central to its identity and that of its members. Therefore, it is essential to understand the nature of the Reform movement in America, if we are to place Temple Shalom in its proper context.

From the start, the Reform movement made the greatest concerted effort to bridge the tradition of the past and the demands of the modern age.[3] Its guiding goal was to preserve Judaism by adapting it to the realities of the modern world. Although it was born in Germany, its greatest development has taken place in the United States.

As in Europe, the original calls for reform in America concentrated more on aesthetics than ideology. These were motivated by the desire to change the character of the traditional service so as to conform more readily to Western tastes. In effect, this meant a critique of traditional worship style and the introduction of decorum into the synagogue.

In general, reforms were gradually adopted in otherwise traditional congregations. Those congregations that embraced Reform from their inception usually grew out of societies, called "Reform-Vereine", which were formed with the purpose of giving expression to the doctrines of Reform. When strong enough, they organized themselves into congregations.

The Reform movement, we may recall, was heir to the Enlightenment. As such, it was committed to liberalism and its ideological principles of rationality, individualism, personal freedom, and faith in progress. Important, as well, were its postures in favor of universalism, the "brotherhood of man," and Western aesthetics.

Sociologically, Reform paved the way for acculturation into Western society and, most clearly, into American culture. Many leaders of Reform, in fact, saw the future of Judaism tied to American society and made valiant efforts to bring about an identity between Judaism and Americanism. For example, Isaac M. Wise, a major figure in the rise of the American Reform movement, saw the American Constitution as "Mosaism in action" (Bamberger 1949, 15).

Another effort in cultural adaptation is expressed by the fact that American Protestantism became the model of Reform synagogal architecture, worship service, and aesthetics. Rabbis became known as ministers and assumed many of the functions associated with

Protestant clergymen, such as priestly and pastoral responsibilities.

The early leadership of the movement was European-born. Many came to the United States in search of more open religious frontiers, for while reforms had proliferated in Europe, strong limitations were set by overarching communal organizations that prevailed there. Leaders ranged from conservative to radical in their reformist convictions; they shared, however, a commitment to reason over "ceremonialism," progress over allegedly dated traditions, the "needs of the times" over ancient preoccupations.

Isaac M. Wise emerged as the great organizer and unifier of the movement. More practical than ideological in temperament, he initially had no desire to create a separate movement in American Judaism. His goal was to forge unity among the various ideological persuasions then current among American rabbis. That was his aim when he founded the Union of American Hebrew Congregations in 1873 and the Hebrew Union College in 1875. He was willing to part company with traditional colleagues only when joint conferences failed. Such a break occurred with the emergence of a Reform platform at the Pittsburgh Conference of 1885.

While there was no consensus regarding the Pittsburgh Platform by those attending the conference, this document nonetheless is believed to express the prevailing tone of opinion among reformers of that and subsequent generations (Philipson 1931, 357). In every way, the Platform is an expression of modernizing efforts. (In the following discussion of the Pittsburgh Platform, all citations of the Platform are to be found in Plaut 1965, 33–34.) The reformers begin with a view of Judaism as an evolutionary religion, one whose merits must be measured by rational scrutiny. Universalistic convictions, as well, inform the Platform in significant ways, frequently self-consciously contrasted with dismissed particularistic positions.

For the reformers, Judaism was "no longer a nation but a religious community" (Plaut 1965, 34). The assumption that had informed all of Jewish life for millenia was therefore dismissed, by changing the stress of Jewishness from national or ethnic dimensions to solely that of a religion with universalistic commitments. In part at least, this position was taken to avert the charge of dual allegiance, a charge that had already been leveled against modernizing Jews in Europe. Arguing that "America is our Zion," reformers felt that the traditional hope for the arrival of a personal Messiah who would restore the Jewish people to Zion was an anachronistic idea. The Messianic idea had such a profound hold on the Jewish imagination, however, that the reformers reinterpreted its meaning rather than dismissing it altogether. In the modern era "of universal culture of heart and intellect," they therefore called for "the realization of Israel's great Messianic hope for the establishment of the kingdom of truth, justice, and peace for all men" (Plaut 1965, 34). The move was thus made from the particularism of the Jewish restoration to the salvation of all humanity.

Also reinterpreted was the traditional concept that the Jews had been exiled from the land of Israel for their sinful acts. Instead, to legitimize another universalistic conviction, the reformers suggested that the exile or Diaspora indeed had been part of a divine scheme, namely, the institution of the "mission of Israel." Having access to the precepts of ethical monotheism—including the unity of God and divine moral commandments—Jews were now seen to have the responsibility to spread the truth to the world, to serve as "a light unto the nations." Consequently, through example, Jews would accomplish their mission precisely by living in the various nations of the world. Such an idea precluded a pro-Zionist position. Universalism overshadowed nationalism, which at that time was the manifestation of Jewish particularism.

A commitment to the prophetic tradition in Judaism became the mark of the Reform movement. Social justice was seen to be the goal of Jewish teachings. At the same time, ceremonial life became evaluated by modern standards:

> We recognize in the Mosaic legislation a system of training the Jewish people for its mission during its national life in Palestine, and to-day we accept as binding only the moral laws and maintain only such ceremonies as elevate and sanctify our lives, but *reject all such as are not adapted to the views and habits of modern civilization*. (Plaut 1965, 34; emphasis added)

The reformers argued, for example, that laws regulating diet and dress were dated, products of another era, as "they fail to impress the modern Jew with a spirit of priestly holiness; their observance in our days is apt rather to obstruct than to further modern spiritual elevation" (Plaut 1965, 34). The "spirit of the age," infused by reason, was contrasted with so-called legalism. Again and again, contrasts were drawn between "inner religiosity" and "outer formalism" or between "the principle of sincerity" and "empty formalism" (Agus 1954, 64).

It is clear, therefore, that the criteria for the reformers were modern standards, those of reason, progress, and goodness of fit with modern and American tastes and ideological inclinations. Worship, personal observance, and philosophical attitudes among Reform Jews reflected these proclivities. A staunch anti-Zionist posture was sustained for generations in Reform circles; social activism, including interfaith dialogue and activity, flourished; and Reform Jews increasingly saw themselves as part of a religion, rather than members of an ethnic or national group.

In adapting to modern times, religious observances and ancient traditions were frequently changed or eliminated. For example, dietary laws were eschewed; in some cases Sunday was adopted as the Jewish Sabbath to fit more readily into American religious cultural life; and a variety of modifications in worship style were introduced. These modifications included the elimination of head covering and prayer shawls, the disappearance of the daily minyan (public prayer by a quorum of at least ten Jewish males over thirteen years of age) service, the abolition of the practice of calling congregants to bless the Torah, and the substitution of confirmation for the bar mitzva ceremony (Agus 1954, 59).

It is important to note that these changes were not facile capitulations to modern demands by people only mildly committed to Jewish survival. On the contrary, Reform leaders as a group were passionately devoted to the continuation of Judaism, but to a Judaism that was viewed as an evolutionary, changing, dynamic faith, one capable of indefinite development and expansion. Its only enduring essence was seen to be the "God-idea," the principle of ethical monotheism. This is the conception that "God is one and ethical in essence, that mankind is one in responsibility and destiny, that the human soul is immortal, and that the perfect society of peace and justice will ultimately be founded" (Agus 1954, 60–61).

In keeping with the liberal humanism that was the reformers' nineteenth-century German legacy, the individual, as opposed to the tradition, became the seat of authority. Reason was, of course, the tool of evaluation and selection. The individual Jew finally had to decide on those elements of the faith that were personally meaningful, intelligible, and important. Individualism in this way superseded communal authority.

Historical, rather than ideological, forces brought about a change in the position of so-called classical Reform. The influx of East

European Jews into America, beginning with the mass migrations of 1880, influenced the course of the Reform movement. These immigrants brought into the then Reform majority a need for traditional and nationalistic emphasis in ritual and ideology. Major events in the twentieth century, including the two world wars and, more particularly, the Nazi Holocaust, shook the Reform nineteenth-century faith in progress and humanity. Reform's adulation of the spirit of the age, universalism, and rationalism faded in the face of world crisis. The persecution and annihilation of European Jewry and the establishment of the State of Israel likewise cemented a renewed commitment to Jewish peoplehood and, in time, to Zionism.

These shifts in the Reform movement led to an effort to find a balance between universalism and particularism. Two documents of the Central Conference of American Rabbis (CCAR) express moves toward such desired balance. The first, known as the Columbus Platform, was issued in 1937. The second is a more recent product, the "Centenary Perspective" adopted by the CCAR in 1976 in honor of the one hundred-year anniversary of the founding of the Union of American Hebrew Congregations and the Hebrew Union College.

By 1937, America had become the center of Diaspora Jewry; Zionism was a religious and political force; antisemitism was building in Europe, with Hitler already in power; and a new world war was in the making. (In the following dicussion of the Columbus Platform, all citations of the Platform are to be found in Plaut 1965, 96–99).

The Columbus Platform was written in the context of these developments. It retains intact some convictions from the earlier Pittsburgh Platform—such as the belief that Judaism expresses universal truths, that the essence of Judaism is the doctrine of one God, that social justice is a major Jewish obligation. But it departs from these in a variety of ways, most specifically by leaning towards particularistic assertions.

In the first place, the Torah, "both written and oral," is seen to enshrine "Israel's ever-growing consciousness of God and of the moral law." Seen as "a depository of permanent spiritual ideals, the Torah remains the dynamic source of the life of Israel" (Plaut 1965, 97). Apart from this important nod to tradition, the Platform makes two major declarations that support a more particularistic understanding of Judaism. Although reaffirming the centrality of religion for Judaism ("Judaism is the soul of which Israel is the body"), Jewish peoplehood is affirmed, as well. It also reverses the previous anti-Zionist stance.

A turn away from strict rationalism is seen in the return to greater ceremonialism. The Conference's previously antiritualistic tenor is changed, as the Platform suggests that

> Judaism as a way of life requires in addition to its moral and spiritual demands, the preservation of the Sabbath, festivals and Holy Days, the retention and development of such customs, symbols and ceremonies as possess inspirational value, the cultivation of distinctive forms of religious art and music and the use of Hebrew, together with the vernacular, in our worship and instruction. (Plaut 1965, 99)

During the same year, the Union of American Hebrew Congregations passed a resolution calling for the restoration of traditional symbols and customs, as well as the use in synagogues of Jewish music sung by Jewish singers and, if possible, by cantors. A few years later a revised version of the Reform prayer book, the *Union Prayer Book for Jewish Worship* (1956), was issued; the changes were basically away from the extreme position of classical Reform (Glazer 1972, 104).

The "Centenary Perspective," issued in 1976, reflects the orientation of Reform Judaism of the last forty years, as it affirms at the same time some major commitments of Reform since its inception. (In the following discussion, all citations of the "Centenary Perspective" are to be found in "Reform Judaism, A Centenary Perspective" 1977, 7-11). An old Reform conviction, for example, is reflected in the statement that "Jewish obligation begins with the informed will of every individual" ("Reform Judaism" 1977, 7). That is, the individual, as the center and final authority in the Reform movement, prevails. Eugene Borowitz, chairperson of the committee that drafted the "Centenary Perspective" and a foremost spokesperson for Reform Judaism today, writes, "Everyone also agrees that the believing, knowledgeable, self-determining individual is the basis of Reform Judaism" (1977, 60). He adds, however, that Reform "now sees individuality as having greater dimension and focuses much of its attention on Jewish peoplehood" (ibid., 149). The Reform movement now suggests that the individual and the people are interdependent entities.

Going beyond the Columbus Platform in its commitment to particularism, the "Centenary" principles suggest that Jews, by birth or conversion "constitute an uncommon union of faith and peoplehood. Born as Hebrews in the ancient Near East, we are bound together like all ethnic groups by language, land, history, culture and institutions" ("Reform Judaism" 1977, 8). Religion, however, remains at the heart of being Jewish. One might suggest that today Reform Jews are sufficiently secure with their legitimate place in American society that they can embrace the particularism of ethnic identification. Certainly the development and celebration of ethnic pluralism in America in recent decades have been factors in the positive turn toward particularism by Reform Judaism.

A turn toward traditionalism in religious practice is also in evidence in the "Centenary Perspective," as it is in Reform Jewish life at large. In a statement that articulates a new balance between universalism and particularism as a goal of Reform Judaism, the Perspective suggests:

> The past century has taught that the claims made upon us may begin with our ethical obligations but they extend to many aspects of Jewish living, including: creating a Jewish home centered on family devotion; life-long study; private prayer and public worship; daily religious observance; keeping the Sabbath and the holy days; celebrating the major events of life; involvement with the synagogue and community; and other activities which promote the survival of the Jewish people and enhance its existence. ("Reform Judaism" 1977, 9)

Significantly, this statement follows:

> Within each area of Jewish observance Reform Jews are called upon to confront the claims of Jewish tradition, however differently perceived, and to exercise their individual autonomy, choosing and creating on the basis of commitment and knowledge. (ibid.)

Hence diversity and ideological pluralism, another longstanding Reform principle, are reiterated, but now in relationship to *traditional* claims. The survival of a meaningful Judaism, one based on knowledge and active involvement, is seen as the responsibility of the Reform Jew. The old Reform obligation toward social justice and the prophetic tradition—action in behalf of universalistic principles and ends—has now gained a particularistic component, as well.

Correspondingly, a turn toward traditionalism, through the reappropriation of ritualistic forms, has taken place in Reform synagogues in the last decade or two. Rutman suggests that the contemporary Jew no longer has to undergo acculturation into the American system, that there is now freedom in Reform

> to experiment Jewishly. Part of the experimentation is in the area of ritual and custom, often a "playing at" being traditional without accepting the assumptions and beliefs of the tradition, often a sincere expression of a desire to identify with Jews who have been or are traditional. (Rutman 1977, 90)

While the return to tradition in these ways is generally applauded, a proviso is frequently expressed:

> While Reform is turning toward the tradition, it is also deeply committed not to be undifferentiatingly subservient to it, and it is especially committed to creating its own way which would become part of the traditional continuum. (Polish 1974, 22)

In effect, such a statement reaffirms Reform's devotion to freedom of thought and independence from externally imposed authority.

The return to the tradition is manifested in a variety of ways. During religious services at Reform synagogues, increasing numbers of people choose to wear ritual garb. In addition, the new Reform prayerbook, *Gates of Prayer*, published in 1975 and widely used, clearly leans in a traditional direction. Hebrew is now increasingly included in the service, frequently in response to congregational demands. The Central Conference of American Rabbis in recent years has published books and manuals for religious home use by Reform Jews, such as the *Gates of the House* (1977) (a home prayerbook), *A Shabbat Manual* (1972), *Gates of Mitzvah: A Guide to the Jewish Life Cycle* (Maslin, 1979), and *Gates of the Seasons: A Guide to the Jewish Year* (Knobel, 1983). All of these encourage the performance of traditional religious actions.

Undoubtedly the return to tradition reflects a move away from the strict rationalsim of classical Reform and a celebration of the non-rational, emotional aspects of religious experience. The Columbus Platform already signalled this move, but a hearty exploration of the tradition has taken place only in recent years. Also foreshadowed in the Columbus Platform, Reform Judaism today fully and enthusiastically supports the State of Israel. Reform Jews, in other words, almost universally are committed Zionists.

The issues that Reform Judaism has dealt with since its inception have always been related to the tension between universalism and particularism. In its early years, universalism was the favored pole, with staunch support for rationalism, universalistic social ethics, anti-ritualism, and antinationalism. In recent years, the scale has tipped the other way, pehaps as pluralism has become enshrined in American Judaism in general and celebrated in American culture as a whole. A turn to tradition and particularistic interests has supplanted in part the former concern with social justice and other humanistic expressions of social activism. Concern with peoplehood, including the State of Israel, is more central for Jews in America today than a preoccupation with Americanism. Certainly the ideological accents of the Reform movement reflect to a great degree the larger American cultural situation. We have moved as a nation from the ideology of the melting pot to a celebration of ethnic pluralism.

In response to the current posture of Reform Judaism, Borowitz writes:

> In our present Jewish mood, I cannot judge whether the danger of equating Torah with tribalism is greater than that of equating it with individual creativity. . . it is the balance among the beliefs which is critical. Reform Judaism is committed to individualism, peoplehood, and the service of God. Undue emphasis on any one of those beliefs leads to a skewed doctrine of Torah. (1977, 153–54)

The tensions between particularism and universalism are therefore far from resolved. Manifestations of each orientation have been current in various phases of American Judaism. Since Reform Judaism has been a religious orientation highly susceptible to cultural demands, the surrounding American situation will dictate in part which pole of the tension receives accentuation at any one point. The balance will also be defined by the extent to which American Reform Jews self-consciously commit themselves to specific ideological and programmatic positions in years to come.

THREE

Ideology and Identity

Groups express their beliefs, values, and attitudes in a variety of ways. A community's ideology—as these elements together might be called—serves to define social meanings for its members.[1] It presents a world view—a particular reading of reality—and calls for the embrace of certain values. In doing so, an ideology serves to cultivate group loyalties, since shared values and ideas help to create collective social definitions and to focus commitment. In this way, a link is found between ideology and identity.

At Temple Shalom, ideology is articulated through several means: by the clergy, in written statements of institutional conviction, through positions taken by formal subgroups, and in informal discussion. These statements raise important implications for the Jewish identity of the institution, as such, and for the identity of its members.

Liberalism

Liberalism constitutes the core of Temple Shalom's ideology. As we have seen, the emergence of the Reform movement occurred in the face of rapidly changing conditions for Jews entering modernity. The Reform ideology shared with other ideologies the tendency to arise during times of social stress and cultural transition. Liberalism was at the center of classical Reform ideology, not surprising since liberal philosophy, in fact, can be considered the Western ideology of modernization par excellence. Its stress on rationality, personal freedom and individualism, progress, universalism, and pluralism reflects the collapse of external authority structures as the individual gains centrality in the modernizing process. In addition, a prophetic interpretation of Judaism fortified Reform's nineteenth-century liberalism, giving it a strong orientation toward social justice and social activism. The American context supported all these tendencies.

We have seen, however, that the Reform movement as a whole has revised its original commitments to allow for a greater degree of particularism (including support for Zionism and ethnocultural, as well as religious definitions of Judaism), traditional ritualism, and an increased sensitivity to the emotional, symbolic, and spiritual components of the religious experience.

In significant ways, Temple Shalom has resisted this retraditionalizing tendency, reflecting to some degree classical Reform proclivities and, by extension, a continuing modernizing agenda. The synagogue's constitution, last amended in 1976, provides a useful entry into Temple Shalom's ideology. It reads in part:

> The purpose of this Congregation shall be to worship God in accordance with the faith of Reform Judaism; to cultivate a love and understanding of the Jewish heritage; to bring nearer the Kingdom of God on earth through the emphasis of the principles of Righteousness, Justice and Love to all the peoples of the world; and to stimulate an awareness of our responsibilities as Jews to the community in which we live. As Americans of Jewish faith we are dedicated to the achievement of a Judaism that contributes to the upbuilding and maintaining of the Biblical ideals inherent in our free America; a Judaism that will aid us to become spiritually sensitive and morally strong human beings; a Judaism that draws its inspiration from the priceless traditions of our American democratic heritage. We have allegiance to no country other than the United States of America but are mindful of the bonds of kinship with our co-religionists throughout the world, and the obligation to discharge our responsibilities to those of our faith who live beyond our borders.

Even a superficial analysis of this statement reveals that key concepts of classical Reform Judaism inform the stated goals of this congregation. "The Kingdom of God on earth," "Americans of Jewish faith," "allegiance to no country other than the United States of America" all readily reflect familiar refrains from classical Reform. Some of these positions, most particularly the heavy-handed Americanism implied here, are now dated even at Temple Shalom and would probably cause embarrassment to some of the members. However, as we shall see, the commitment to Reform Judaism as such, to the prophetic and universalistic tradition, and to the embrace of Western truths, as well as the Jewish heritage, still stand firm.

A generally agreed-upon and rather specific ideology appears to reign at Temple Shalom. The congregation sees it principally as a reflection of the senior rabbi's philosophy. The other rabbi typifies it in this way:

> [It] includes things like racial justice, openness in religion, social action, a diversity and pluralism in the community, organizational independence, seriousness about Jewish ideas (even if we don't believe them), respect for the Jewish Tradition (with a capital "T") and liberation from many of those traditions (with a small "t"). (All field note quotations may be found in Furman 1978.)

This ideology places ethics at the heart of Judaism. Other religious emphases or ritualistic considerations are consequently underplayed and sometimes devalued.

Conceding that "the confrontation with the holy or the sacred is not a familiar category in my theology," one of the rabbis sermonized that doing justice is far more important than following the ritual commandments. He argued that, although both are needed, being ritually pure is useless without the ethical component. More frequently, however, the ritual prescriptions of traditional Judaism are seen in contradistinction to the activist social ethic propounded here.

The call for the pursuit of social justice on a universal scale results in an "outward" as opposed to an "inward" view of Judaism. As one congregant suggests, "There is a commitment to basic human rights, a commitment to experience, understanding and involvement with people other than ourselves. This is a commitment that is not just an inward-looking Judaism." Another individual expresses this sentiment as follows:

> There is a stress placed on the experience of Jewishness as it relates to the outside world, with less stress on the development of the self as a Jew. . . .The effect that Temple Shalom has had on me is that it has opened me to try to combine Judaism with the outside world.

And a young woman who grew up as a member of Temple Shalom suggests that during that time

> the emphasis at Temple Shalom was decidedly ethical . . . in nature; very little of it was "Jewish." For instance, there was little training

as to what is going on in the services. Instead, activities included going to a school in _____ [a Black ghetto], visiting a monastery for a weekend, going to a Catholic service.

More so-called Jewish options are available to religious school students today. But the reappropriation of the Jewish tradition and the increasing interest in Jewish practice and knowledge that has been embraced by the Reform movement in recent years is often interpreted at Temple Shalom as a capitulation to the privatism and narcissism of contemporary America. For example, in a sermon, one of the rabbis critiques the self-centeredness of the 1970s in light of the many societal problems still unsolved:

> It is so much more comfortable to retreat from this insanity. . .to follow the rise and fall of the market and wonder what it means; to find solace in a better forehand, in a smaller waist, a lower cholesterol count, the newest boutique, or *something Jewish.* (emphasis added)

Temple Shalom's ideology is decidedly in the prophetic tradition of Reform Judaism, yet it is admittedly eclectic in its content. Borrowing from Western liberalism, it celebrates personal freedom and diversity of opinion. Arguing for a "defense of pluralism in Jewish life today," one of the rabbis states, "I seem to thrive best as a rabbi and a Jew in an atmosphere of freedom, and my congregants should have the same options."

Indeed, a characteristic of Temple Shalom universally applauded by its members is its commitment to the individual's complete freedom "to be self-defining as a Jew," to freely choose those beliefs and practices he or she finds meaningful. As one congregant puts it, "the lack of dogma about Judaism and Jewish expression has created an atmosphere of openness. . .to pursue and find. . .individual identities."

The rabbis' public assertions are occasionally tinted with a measure of cynicism and a good dose of reality regarding human limitations. Nonetheless, they still subscribe to the liberal faith in social progress and human perfectibility:

> I am not completely sure what it means to be created in the Divine Image, but I sense that I learned something about the meaning of that old expression recently, when I saw ancient frontiers of ignorance succumbing to the disciplined assaults of human beings! What

does it all mean? At least this much: Let those who say that cancer
is incurable, that war will always be with us, and that nothing can
be done about poverty, be silent. Now, at last, we should all know
that they are wrong, refuted by the power of those created but little
lower than the angels.

The need to be active in the world, to work toward societal amelio-
ration and social equality, to eradicate pain and anguish wherever
it is found is therefore seen to be all the more pressing given the
possibility and responsibility of bringing about the Kingdom of God
or its human counterpart.

One of the rabbis is fond of saying that "the world needs Jews"
to prod the conscience of the world. Hence, Judaism is seen, "not
as something divorced from life, not separated from politics or business,
not simply religious. Judaism is part of everything you do." Or, as
another member suggests, "The commitment of Jewish idealism to
social change is the primary purpose of religion. . .otherwise religion
is useless."

Egalitarianism—an aspect of liberalism—is considered part of
Temple Shalom's ideology, and concrete examples are repeatedly cited
to illustrate this commitment. No memorial plaques or lights adorn
the building, nor are seats, particular rooms, or funds identified by
a specific donor, as is common in American synagogues. This attempt
to equalize the importance of all individuals is not intended, however,
to diminish the value of the individual, as such. As one member
contends, "While [Temple Shalom] prohibits individuality from a
material perspective. . .it exalts the individuality of every person. I
can't think of any time when I haven't been politely listened to."

The synagogue sees itself as "an equal opportunity temple," one
committed to "socialist principles." Undoubtedly, the senior rabbi's
socialist convictions during the early years of Temple Shalom were
influential in this regard. Dues structure differs from that of most
congregations. A fair share system (in which dues are based on percentage of income) prevails, instead of the usual set fee that often precludes
membership of people without means. In this way, Temple Shalom
has made a commitment to democratizing its membership. (Although
this system has created financial difficulties and is often the subject
of heated discussion as to its practicability, the ethical principle at
stake is never questioned.)

Suspicious of systems and their rigidity, the rabbis are unsystematic in their philosophy; they are committed to a pluralistic orientation to religion. One rabbi suggests that they are "old fashioned liberals. . . humanists, man- or human being-centered." In developing a philosophy, he adds, "Mine is an effort to use symbols and traditions of the Jewish people *selectively*, to enhance values that are partly rooted in the Jewish tradition and partly derived from the culture in which we live."

On occasion, a conscious selection from the Jewish tradition is used to inform current ethical problems. For example, during a rather unpleasant finance committee meeting, salaries and difficult budgetary matters were discussed. One of the rabbis retorted that he did not see "how the ethics of industry can be contrasted to the ethics of Sinai. . . and applied to the Temple." The implication here is that a synagogue must be submitted to the demands of Sinai, a moral scheme Jewish in content, which transcends the ethics of industry, given its genesis in a divine plane. This type of moral reasoning is rare at Temple Shalom, largely because of the institution's secularistic tendencies. That orientation often discourages the derivation of values from traditionally sacred imperatives.

Far more common is a tendency to identify Judaism with Western liberalism and humanism. As one of the rabbis states,

> I used to agonize over this [issue] because I was accused by some of preaching humanism under the guise of Judaism or of taking secular liberal values out of the secular liberal tradition and dressing them up in Jewish symbolism. I no longer agonize over this question, in part due to my understanding of the dynamics of Jewish history. . . .What has been called Judaism through the ages is actually an amalgam of tradition and other sources.

From this perspective, Jewish values are seen to emerge naturally out of a setting that is Jewish, rather than through a conscious attempt to draw on traditional Jewish sources. Two examples should clarify this process. Arguments over membership dues have plagued the board of trustees for years. The rabbi just cited interprets this problem in the following way:

> I get impatient sometimes. But then I realize that this is a gut Jewish issue going on here. . . more profound than anything I can say from the pulpit. The fiscal integrity of this institution relates to its ability

to be a proud bearer of the Jewish tradition, under the name "synagogue."

When an anniversary celebration with a high admission ticket was planned, a number of people complained that many members would feel excluded. The rabbi's interpretation of this response serves to explicate further his notion of Jewishness:

> When people criticize us, as they did so vociferously about the anni-versary party that we had . . . they are talking about cutting people out of a major community event, catering to the rich . . . criticizing us for dirtying, sullying, diluting the democracy of the Temple . . . that's a Jewish issue they are talking about . . . not in any narrow sense . . . but they are talking about the ethos of this congregation, which we try consistently to make a place that is not just an institu-tion; it is a *synagogue* which also happens to be an institution.

Asked what separates this kind of wrestling from liberal argumen-tation, in general, or from what might go on at a liberal Protestant church, he responded,

> I'm not sure that anything does, except the consciousness that we are a synagogue, not a church. If I were a minister at _____ [a liberal church] and I were at this same meeting, I might say that the principles of Christianity forbid us to do that without at least raising a question. So [the minister] may be looking over his shoulder saying that Jesus, Paul, and the Apostles are looking. And I am thinking over my shoulder—though maybe not consciously— that Amos and Isaiah are looking at us . . . and they talked about selling the needy for corruption in the courts and the lack of integrity in the social system of their time. And don't we, as an institution, if we are to be worthy of that heritage, have the duty to act with honesty and integrity?

The logic of this moral argument seems to suggest that the fact that Temple Shalom is a synagogue makes its values Jewish. A link between liberalism and Judaism is therefore effected by virtue of the fact that the people holding the values are Jews, rather than the intrinsic Jewishness of the values themselves.

At Temple Shalom, liberalism, with its implicit humanism, is identified with the prophetic tradition. Consequently, currently held commitments are authenticated as Jewish. This identification is continually reiterated, in part at least to make present the Jewishness of the expressed values. Sermons, in particular, are continually used in this way, by expressing ethical statements that associate social justice with Judaism. During a bar mitzva sermon, for example, it is not unusual to hear that becoming a man means becoming an independent ethical person who needs to make decisions consistent with the Jewish prophetic tradition, such as doing for others and resisting the appeal of materialism and affluence. A common sentiment is expressed by these words from a rabbi's sermon: "Wherever we act out of love to help diminish the store of human anguish, we assert our power as Jews." To be good Jews, congregants are told to be kind and caring toward one another and to participate in the healing of the whole world. This idea is not uncommon in other Reform synagogues.

Temple Shalom's ideology has been successful in shaping the Jewish identity of its members; in many cases, as has been suggested, this ideology seems to mirror the values that the congregants held before joining. Through its very close identification between Judaism and liberalism, Temple Shalom authenticates as Jewish the members' liberal self-conceptions. As one member states, "Temple Shalom represents for me a place where thoughts and ideas can be expressed, especially liberal ideas, which I equate with being Jewish."

This is a setting of high self-consciousness and reflection. Several members indicate their awareness that Jewish meanings may be attached to liberal commitments in order both to legitimize liberalism and affirm Judaism: "I think that being Jewish reinforces my secular commitments to justice and fairness. It's hard to say which came first . . . it's a chicken/egg dilemma." Congregants who, until joining Temple Shalom, did not have a particularly positive sense of Jewish identity suggest that they now realize that some of their values, such as their concern for social justice or their commitment to pacifism, are "really Jewish values."

One perceptive congregant says, referring to Temple Shalom as a whole, "We tend to emphasize humanitarian goals and ideals that are *consistent* with Jewish teaching . . . [though] not strictly Jewish." Another members adds, "I think the rabbis look to tradition, to Torah, for words that will justify this philosophy. It is important to them, I think, to tie it to the Jewish tradition."

One member suggests that the ideology of Temple Shalom is typified by "innovation" and "nontradition," adding that "there is just enough tradition in its nontradition to legitimize it." Thus, many members are aware that the link between their Judaism and their liberalism is a critical one, and few question its legitimacy. This is probably because they themselves have, for the most part, whole-heartedly embraced this ideology; in fact, it serves as the very content of their Jewish identity. This fact is reflected in congregants' responses to the question, "What does it mean for you to be Jewish?" The following are some representative answers:

> For me to be a Jew is principally an obligation, a commitment to fair play, justice, freedom. It is an obligation: "Thou shall not stand idly by."

> To fight for the things that I believe in is Jewish. All the things that I feel strongly about, such as my liberalism, are Jewish.

> To be Jewish means to be honest, to be fair. It means doing rather than being.

> Being Jewish is related to ethical considerations, such as emphasis on justice, mercy, humanitarianism, responsibility.

> Being Jewish implies a close connection with the Bible, the imple-mentation of the Torah's moral imperatives, obligations in day-to-day life.

Clearly, liberalism and social activism stand at the heart of these views of Judaism. That which falls radically outside of this view is seen as questionably Jewish by some members. A discussion about the giving of the Law at Sinai provides an interesting example. One member felt disturbed that the Ten Commandments were given to Moses in private, for in his opinion, "this is counter to the demo-cratic spirit of the Jewish tradition." In like manner, several people expressed discomfort with the fact that sacrifices were performed in the Temple in Jerusalem and that these were conducted by priests. The cruelty implied by the sacrifice of animals seemed "unJewish" to some, and so did the existence of priests, since "Judaism invites the direct relationship of the individual with God." A final example is the dissatisfaction expressed with the book of Leviticus, which deals largely with ritual prescriptions. Some members, as well as one of the rabbis, have stated that much of this book seems irrelevant to the meaning of Judaism.

These views obviously reveal a specific interpretation of Judaism.

Although clearly many people are able to interpret such passages within a historical context and assign them contextual or symbolic meanings, it is interesting to observe the almost complete identification between Judaism and modern liberalism in the consciousness of many members.

Of particular interest is the general absence of ethnic or traditionally religious meanings associated with Judaism by Temple Shalom members. In fact, many respondents suggest that ethnicity is decidedly not a part of their Jewish identity. This absence is not surprising, however, given the strongly universalistic tenor of Temple Shalom's ideology, which would legislate against the particularism of ethnicity. Active campaigns on behalf of Soviet Jews, for example, have not been conducted at Temple Shalom through the time of this study. Some congregants express the feeling that they more readily identify with a historical link to the Jewish people than with existing Jewish communities in various parts of the world today.

As to the absence of a theological dimension in Jewish identity, this congregant's statement characterizes many other views: "I see Judaism primarily as an ethic as opposed to worshipping of God as such." Similarly, another congregant admits to having difficulty with a concept like "belief in God." She suggests that her children's exposure to the grape boycott in support of the Farm Workers' Union at Temple Shalom was most important to them: "I feel it was much more dramatic than going to Temple on the high holidays. It represented an aspiration for mankind." One of the rabbis, whose sense of Jewishness evolved largely through political involvements in his youth, suggests that "secularism—but one that has quasi-religious meanings—has permeated my approach to Jewishness." Political ideology has furnished these "quasi-religious meanings" to his Jewish identity.

While most congregants with whom I had contact feel that Temple Shalom's ideology expresses their own, one member reveals serious reservations with the ideology as it stands. She suggests that she agrees with its basic premise; nonetheless, she feels that this philosophy "does not go far enough":

> The moral dimension, the ethical base of Judaism, is important to me. This has traditionally involved man's relationship to man, since this is viewed as most important in terms of living. But in recent years, I increasingly have seen that ethical action comes out of a

religious commitment, of a covenant relationship between myself and God... If I talked about this sort of thing with people at Temple Shalom, most likely they would not know what I'm talking about.

This member's perception corresponds to my observations, insofar as the religious dimension as she understands it is neither ideologically nor socially supported by the rabbis or members of Temple Shalom.

Social Activism

Temple Shalom sees itself and is seen by others as an activist congregation, given its ideological commitment to a liberal/prophetic interpretation of Judaism. Its rabbis are known for their participation in a variety of liberal causes, not infrequently causes that are unpopular in the eyes of the larger Jewish community. The congregation has been singularly supportive and respectful of the clergy's postures, even when in disagreement with them.

Many members state that the social activist image of the synagogue motivated them to join Temple Shalom. Others say that what they like best about Temple Shalom is its social activism. The embodiment of such activism is to be found in the synagogue's social action committee. According to the Temple's handbook, that committee

> tries to implement the Jewish ideals of moral responsibility and involvement. Seeking to inform, sensitize or provoke the congregation, this active, concerned group of temple members brings issues of social importance to our attention, encourages cooperation with Jewish and non-Jewish organizations, and sponsors community interest programs. They combine personal participation with education in their efforts to cope with injustices effectively.

During the period of this study, however, social action committee meetings and programs were very poorly attended. During one committee meeting, the disappointed committee members seriously considered the possibility of eliminating the committee, given the lack of general interest in its pursuits. This suggestion was effectively undermined when one member argued that "Temple Shalom without a social action committee is like Judaism without God!" In the passion of the moment, she probably did not realize what an apt metaphor she had selected. For, as we have seen, the commitment to social justice, with its implied commitment to social activism, is at the heart of Temple Shalom's ideology and of its identity as a Jewish institution. The social action image perpetuates this arrangement, giving active validation and content to the ideology. The elimination of the social action committee, however ineffective its programs, would, in fact, threaten the very identity that has been cultivated at Temple Shalom.

A cochair of this committee complained about the lack of real involvement by members in programs of social import that she considers critical. "Why do they maintain this fiction?" she asked. "It would be more honest to do away with the committee than to pretend it is alive and well." What she missed in her evaluation is the critical symbolic function that the social action committee plays at Temple Shalom. The rhetoric about social justice needs a reality base, however weak, to maintain itself. The myth of social activism, as a fulfillment of the liberal/prophetic ideology, is kept alive in part by maintaining the structure that is responsible for activating such ideology. In this manner, the majority of members find a vicarious expression of the ideology they embrace which gives content to their Jewish identity.

Another way members validate their definitions of Jewishness within Temple Shalom is through the activities of their rabbis, who are publicly involved in a variety of social causes. Like the social action committee, therefore, they represent an expression of vicarious Jewish identity for members who subscribe to the synagogue's ideology.

The Jewish Tradition

It has already been suggested that members of Temple Shalom are, on the whole, not a learned group in regard to Judaism. Indeed, many confess to having a very weak Judaic background. Given the universalistic and modernist commitments of Temple Shalom's ideology, the attitude toward the Jewish (rabbinic) tradition is characterized by ambivalence and, occasionally, by hostility.[2] This tradition is seldom explored with attention to content. Rather, it is seen in contradistinction to Temple Shalom's ideology and self-identity, associating it with the premodern Jewish experience or with the practice of Orthodox Jews.

By contrast, congregants see themselves as pluralistic, individualistic, and secularized, in short, as modern members of American society. Yet however vague, selective, or fictitious their conception of the tradition might be, the latter is an important component in the process of identity construction and identity maintenance at Temple Shalom. The following example demonstrates this point.

The Yarmulke Controversy

I select an example from the synagogue's ritual life, since rituals and ritual symbols provide such profound expressions of personal and collective identity and continuity with the past. They therefore serve to communicate values and to establish the individual's place in the collectivity. (See Chapter Four for an elaboration of this point.) Ritual symbols are multivocal (Turner 1967, 50), so they have a multiplicity of possible meanings. How Temple Shalom understands and responds to a particular ritual symbol therefore can tell us a great deal about the congregants' identity as modern Jews. A heated, drawn-out argument over the use of yarmulkes (skullcaps) identifies rather succinctly Temple Shalom's general view of the traditon and the use of that tradition in defining the identity of its members.[3]

Orthodox Jewish males wear yarmulkes at all times as a sign of reverence. Among them, head covering at the synagogue is therefore obligatory. As Jews entered modern society, many uncovered their heads in public as an adaptation to Western style. Mandatory head covering in the synagogue was discontinued by the early Reform movement, and in some synagogues the use of yarmulkes was actually forbidden. However, as we have seen, in recent decades the Reform movement has moved toward the reappropriation of once rejected traditional ritual, and yarmulkes have optionally returned to many Reform synagogues. These are frequently made available at the entrance of the sanctuary for those who wish to wear them.

This is not the case at Temple Shalom. The norm here is the absence of head covering. Neither clergy nor the overwhelming majority of congregants wear yarmulkes during services. At most, a handful of men may be seen with their heads covered at a Sabbath service; very frequently these are guests rather than members.

A controversy began when a congregant complained to the president of the synagogue that she felt "shocked" by his wearing a yarmulke during high holiday services. During services, the president sits on the *bima* (the raised platform in front of the sanctuary). She was willing to allow him the freedom to do what he wished as an

individual, in keeping with liberal commitments. As her representative on the bima, however, she felt offended by his use of the
yarmulke, since she had been brought up in a classical Reform
synagogue where head covering was anathema.

The president took this issue to the synagogue's ritual committee,
where heated debate about this and related issues took place for many
months, with intermittent discussion of the topic occurring among
congregants and members of the board of trustees, as well. Three issues,
in effect, became the subject of discussion: (a) the right of the
president to wear a yarmulke; (b) Temple Shalom's position regarding
the use of yarmulkes during services; and (c) the advisability (or lack
thereof) of making yarmulkes available for those wishing to wear them.

The arguments regarding these issues by clergy and members alike
represent ways in which this community defines itelf as a modern
entity vis-à-vis their conception of the Jewish tradition. The process,
in fact, illustrates mechanisms of separation from the tradition, as well
as means through which their identity remains linked to the tradition. Since identity in some ways is continually being constructed,
the analysis of one such protracted event provides interesting clues
as to the sources and direction of such identity.

As we have seen, Temple Shalom sees itself as a modern and
modernizing synagogue, one committed to dynamism, change, and
openness to the future. This self-image is informed by a self-conscious
commitment to the Reform movement, which arose in reaction against
traditional Judaism. Thus, to the extent that Temple Shalom identifies with the early Reform movement, it places itself against traditionalism. Yarmulkes are therefore associated with the tradition and all
its connotations. Through these discussions, the synagogue was
making a gesture of self-disclosure, for to endorse the use of yarmulkes
and to have them freely accessible represents a public alignment with
a traditional ritual symbol, and by extension, with the presumably
rejected tradition.

An analysis of these discussions reveals a dichotomization between
Temple Shalom's identity and the tradition, a disjunction which serves
as a mechanism of self-definition for this community of modern Jews.
For, while a profound ambivalence toward the tradition is evident
in the life of the synagogue, there is also a pervasive preoccupation
with such tradition. In a sense, it could be said that Temple Shalom
cannot live with the tradition, but it cannot live without it either.
In this dynamic, one can perhaps understand the meaning that Jewish

identity holds for this community of persons which is alienated from the tradition of the past but, at the same time, is groping for an identity it can nonetheless call Jewish.

The tension between modernity and tradition may be briefly observed through an examination of the principal dichotomous pairs that emerge out of the discussions regarding the yarmulke:

1. Temple Shalom sees itself as committed to personal freedom, whereas the tradition is viewed as coercive and potentially threatening to the individual's freedom. Thus, the suggestion to provide yarmulkes outside the sanctuary was finally voted down on the grounds that individuals would feel coerced to wear them. A suggestion to place them in an unobtrusive place, to be available to those persons who ask for them, was finally passed; however, a related suggestion—to make such availability known to the congregation through the Temple's bulletin—was not approved. In the last analysis, in this context freedom of choice favors those who choose from modernity over those who choose from the tradition. The nonwearer's rights were seen as more fundamental than the potential wearer's. One member captured the general feeling when he said, "If someone wants to wear a yarmulke, let him bring his own."

2. While the rabbis are tolerant toward those who choose to wear yarmulkes, they also refer to yarmulke-wearing and other traditional expressions as "mindless traditionalism." In contrast, they see themselves and the Reform movement in which they were schooled as champions of rationalism. The tradition is seen as mindless because its embrace is construed as unconsidered, not thought through and evaluated, but done somewhat under compulsion. One rabbi suggests that the disappointment with science and reason in recent years has led to the "escape from freedom" into "cultic tribalism," an escape to traditional structure, certainty, and security. Rationalism is thus seen as the rightful modern option, one open to the challenges, the changes, and the diversity of the present. By contrast, the tradition is seen as static and closed off to the dynamic calls of global concerns.

3. Related to this is the perception that Temple Shalom is committed to activism in the world, that is, to a social conscience that ideally leads to universalistic endeavors. Traditional concerns are thought to symbolize inwardness and privatism, the "cultivation of one's own garden," in short, particularism and parochialism. Discussions about yarmulkes are therefore denigrated by some since they represent concerns that do not merit time, effort, and, least of all,

anguish and potential congregational schism. They are seen as ridiculous, or, in the words of one rabbi, "yarmulkes are in the realm of *meshugas*," the realm of craziness or the absurb.

4. Finally, Temple Shalom sees itself as having a different aesthetic from that found in the tradition. One member, for instance, said that he has a negative attitude to yarmulkes because he finds them "unattractive, silly looking. A yacht cap would be better," he concluded. Several members have suggested that they can appreciate other ritual symbols, such as the Torah or the *menora* (a ritual candelabrum), only if they are aesthetically pleasing or "well put up."

This kind of dichotomization is evident in many facets of congregational life and is not restricted to the yarmulke issue alone. Sermons frequently discuss how the synagogue departs from the tradition. An extended adult education series, entitled "Tradition and Freedom: Being a Jew Today," was offered. Lecture series by the rabbis also have dealt with this topic, as have ongoing educational groups, such as the weekly Torah study group.

This preoccupation with the tradition thus betrays a need to deal with it in some way, however formalistically that might be. As mentioned, the tradition is often treated unidimensionally, either out of ignorance or with selective intent. This formal characterization serves a functional end: to give shape to a modern identity with a weakened Jewish content whose form contrasts radically with that attributed to the tradition. The tradition is therefore addressed through typification and dichotomization, but addressed it is nonetheless.

This continual dialogue with the tradition allows the Jews of Temple Shalom to assert their uniqueness, distinctiveness, and modernity, on the one hand. On the other hand, they can affirm simultaneously a link, however complex, fragmentary, or abrasive, with the tradition, a link that allows them to remain firmly—if never fully comfortably—within the boundaries of the Jewish world. As Smith suggests, "For a given group at a given time to choose this or that mode of interpreting their tradition is to opt for a *particular* way of relating themselves to their historical past and social present" (cited in Neusner 1977, 16; emphasis added).

The Question of Jewish Content

Ambivalence toward their Judaism is not an unusual characteristic of modern American Jews, given their twin desires of becoming fully acculturated to American society and of preserving their particular heritage. A related phenomenon, and one that contributes to the problem of ambivalence, is the ambiguity frequently associated by contemporary Jews with the meaning of Judaism and Jewishness. It is difficult to resolve ambivalence when the very meaning of one's Jewishness is unclear. As was mentioned in Chapter One, the compartmentalization of Jewish identity (into religion, race, culture, and nationality) was a by-product of Jewish modernization.

Various responses to this problem have been offered. From the religious camp, it is suggested that unambiguous and authentic Jewish identity can only emerge when the religious dimension is placed at the heart of Jewish identity. Among ardent Zionists, nationalism seems to occupy center stage in their Jewish identitites. A variety of Jews display an ethnic Jewish identity, frequently expressed through a commitment to Jewish peoplehood (K'lal Yisrael); efforts on behalf of oppressed Jews in various parts of the world are expressions of such commitment. Finally, the secularist-Yiddishist movement might be mentioned, which, though no longer powerful, at one time was thought to provide countless Jewish immigrants with a secure and unambiguous Jewish identity.

At Temple Shalom the absence of a wholehearted commitment to any one element of the tradition—religious, nationalistic, ethnic, or cultural—results in an ambiguous sense of Jewish identity.[4] Secondly, the universalistic and modernist commitments of the members of Temple Shalom a priori set themselves against an appreciation of an ancient and frequently particularistic tradition, as has been seen in the yarmulke discussion. The stress on individual choice, in the absence of traditional grounding or knowledge, leaves the individual free to construct his or her identity but rather unclear as to what the options are.

The close identification between liberalism and Judaism brings difficulties, as well as benefits. One congregant who was brought up as a member of Temple Shalom had her first encounter with a more traditional Jewish orientation when she went to a weekend retreat in her late teens, a retreat sponsored by another Jewish institution. Exposed to religious and ritualistic expressions she had never encountered at Temple Shalom, she went through a period of confusion trying to sort out what was meaningfully Jewish for her. She cheerfully arrived at the following conclusion: "I'm Jewish, but I'm also a Temple

Shalom-er!" Faced with a different set of criteria for what is Jewish, the authenticity of Temple Shalom's vision broke down. She was forced to dichotomize between her Jewishness and her commitment to Temple Shalom, as if her identity as a member of Temple Shalom were not a Jewish one. By doing so, she called into question the soundness of Temple Shalom's view of Judaism. Whether or not this member's perceptions were correct is immaterial; however, the very fact that she raised this issue is of importance in this analysis. It points to the precariousness of the definition of Jewishness—and, by extension, to the precariousness of the Jewish identity—that potentially emerges from Temple Shalom's ideology.

Earlier in this chapter, I presented one of the rabbi's perceptions that what takes place at Temple Shalom, regardless of particular content, is Jewish, inasmuch as it arises from a specific ethos, that of a synagogue. For the young member just cited, it is clear that this definition is insufficient. More content is necessary for a clear conception of Judaism to stand on its own. I have discussed the centrality of the liberal/prophetic tradition in forming Temple Shalom's ideology, and I have cited the merits of such a link found by members who either had no Jewish identity prior to joining or felt alienated from Judaism or Jewishness for a variety of reasons. The openendedness of the definition of Judaism and Jewishness at Temple Shalom, in fact, acts as a kind of port of entry, or reentry, into Judaism for those people. But its very flexibility can be distressing, when it comes to comparing its meaning with that which others assign to Jewish identity or in transmitting this meaning to one's children. The latter raises the issue of Jewish continuity, an issue of great moment today in the larger Jewish community.

Members were surprisingly optimistic when asked what they felt was the future of Judaism and, more particularly, whether they were concerned about the survival of Judaism. Many seemed to feel that, since Jews had survived for millenia, there was no question but that Judaism would continue. Few members addressed the nature of this Judaism in the future, that is, the question of content. Nor did people ponder how survival would be secured. The certainty about Jewish survival was more on the level of a faith commitment. One respondent, for example, felt "confident that, left to our own devices, we'll survive."

An opposite sentiment was expressed by another member:

I feel rather pessimistic about this. A strong religious thrust is missing today. There is nothing left to knit the group together as Orthodox Judaism used to do. Reform Judaism almost invites you to drop out; there is too much freedom, no directives. A gut-level feeling is missing.

This respondent was raising the question of content when he made the allusion to religion having knit the group together, an observation reminiscent of Durkheim (1964). In the absence of a strong religious center and the recognition of Temple Shalom's secularism, a void is perceived by this congregant; what is missing for him is the substance of what constitutes Judaism, the glue that attracts one to a tradition and secures one's commitment to it. In fact, one of the rabbis felt that the issue of content needs critical attention in the life of Temple Shalom. Suggesting that the synagogue is a "sleeping giant," he argued that

we have no excuses for *not* dealing with deep questions, for avoiding the gut issues of Jewish life, such as what is the nature of our faith? What do we believe in and not believe in? Why do we believe? How do we overcome the rigidity of our agnosticism? How do we reappropriate Jewish experiences? In regard to the religious school, how do we translate our religious school into important religious learning? We need to deal with these ideological issues now. We have the luxury and the necessity to do all this. The rabbis should be able to articulate what they believe and see. I see us on the cutting edge of religious development. . . . We are emancipated Jews whose Judaism doesn't have to be totally institutional or organizational in expression but should have content. Defining and developing content is important. So "sleeping giant" refers to our unfulfilled potentials.

Despite such statements of desired change, Temple Shalom, its ideology, and its identity have remained fairly stable for years, in continuity with its own traditions.

Labeling is a process that undergirds all identity construction mechanisms that have been discussed in the course of this chapter. We have seen that identity is structured through an identification of Judaism with liberalism/prophetism and, by extension, with a social activist image. Identity is also forged by pitting present self-image against a formalistic perception of the tradition, using the latter as a backdrop against which a modern Judaism can be defined.

The identification with the Reform movement is a primary and much rehearsed association at Temple Shalom. By calling themselves Reform, the rabbis or members not only define who they are ideologically but mark their boundaries, as well, separating from non-Reform and joining with other Reform Jews (see Strauss 1959, 15–30). Naming is a normal human activity, and as such its practice, in and of itself, is not particularly interesting or provocative. The great frequency with which people at Temple Shalom name themselves as Reform Jews, however, perhaps bespeaks an identity that needs frequent reaffirmation, an ongoing restatement of who one is and what are the boundaries of one's identity. As one member put it, "It is a source of great pride to some members *just how Reform* Temple Shalom is."

The repeated emphasis on social activism, discussed earlier, plays a similar function, for here, too, naming serves to give substance to an otherwise unclear identity. The preoccupation with the Jewish tradition, discussed sketchily and often negatively, is an expression of labeling and identity construction, as well, since it tells congregants who they are not. Finally, an undercurrent of self-deprecating humor about who they are as Jews informs some of the members' self-images at Temple Shalom. One congregant, for example, suggested that people are very "proud of being Jewish, yet concerned with being too Jewish." One member offered that Israeli folk dancing is not done at Temple Shalom because it is "too Jewish." And a congregant was jestingly silenced by another during services when the former sang along with the cantor during a traditional liturgical passage: "Shhh!" said her friend. "You can't do that here. It's too Jewish!"

That one activity or another should be perceived as "too Jewish" certainly bespeaks ambivalence, as the following words from a member suggest: "Once in a while I think I've become too Jewish! I want to be a little less obviously Jewish. I find the overdisplay of Judaism to be embarrassing." While such a statement might be interpreted in a variety of ways, it readily reveals, along with the statements quoted above, a discomfort with particularism and specificity of Jewish meanings. This may partly explain Temple Shalom's unwillingness to provide more clear and unambiguous meanings of what constitutes Jewish identity.

Summary and Conclusions

Ambivalence about Jewish identity is perhaps an inevitable condition of the modern American experience for Jews, since their tendencies toward modernity preclude an unquestioned commitment to a particularistic tradition rooted in the past. The broad characteristics of modernity—secularism, universalism, individualism—have clearly shaped the ideology that informs identity at Temple Shalom.

We have seen that Temple Shalom is ideologically highly selective vis-à-vis the Jewish tradition. Strongly attached to Reform convictions, this synagogue is also selective in regard to that religious movement. In the area of ritual, for example, Temple Shalom differs in some ways from the current thrust of the movement. In addition, it will be recalled, at the heart of Reform ideology is a religious commitment, that is, a concern with God. Secularism has infiltrated Temple Shalom's ideology to a degree where discussion about God is absent. God forms no active part of the motivational base for its ideology, nor is God used in a justificatory way.

Here political liberalism, inheriting the Enlightenment's anti-religious proclivities, finds rooting in a humanistic conviction: that the individual alone must struggle with existential and societal dilemmas. As Bluhm suggests, "Ideology. . . substitutes for religion as a set of ideas that give meaning to human experience as a secular political experience" (1974, 27). Hence, this ideology lacks a transcendental referent in the usual sense of the term, that is, a supernatural reality. Its major components, political liberalism and the prophetic tradition, are linked in ways that serve to give Jewish legitimacy to a modern ideology.

Efforts to derive liberalism from the Jewish religious tradition have been common. But there are convincing arguments that such connections are spurious. Liberal attitudes among modern Jews are far more likely to have emerged out of the Enlightment, the Emancipation, and the political experience of Jews since that period than from the Jewish tradition, as such (Glazer 1972, 136–41; Liebman 1973, 135–59). The continual association made between liberalism and the prophetic tradition, which in effect furnishes the meaning of Judaism at Temple Shalom, is not, however, a contrived invention for this community. Indeed, the identification between these traditions is passionately believed in by clergy and members alike.

This conviction derives in part from the Reform legacy that so strongly supported this interpretation of Judaism. Given the thin content of Jewish identity at Temple Shalom, however, the identification of present conviction with the ancient past can be seen as a mechanism for negotiating a move in identity and valuation from the personal to the transpersonal, from the secular to the sacred. By labeling current, personal values "Jewish," this ideology allows the move from the personal to the collective. A sacralizing of personal identity results in this process, for the liberal values held by the person are invested with transcendent collective meanings, transcending time, space, and personal anomie. The individual and his or her values are rendered part of a larger reality, the Jewish people. So, despite the modern antipathy toward the tradition as a whole evidenced at Temple Shalom, the rooting of political liberalism in the prophets—admittedly selected from tradition—effects an important function. As Gusfield suggests,

> Tradition is not something out there, always over one's shoulder. It is rather plucked, created, and shaped to present needs and aspirations in a given historical situation. Men refer to aspects of the past as tradition in grounding their present actions in some legitimating principle. In this fashion, tradition becomes an ideology, a program of action in which it functions as a goal or as a justificatory base. (1967, 358)

As argued earlier, while the tradition is apprehended in a complex and often mixed manner at Temple Shalom, it nonetheless is addressed continually. It functions to provide a boundary for identity, by "grounding...present actions in some legitimating principle." (ibid.) And indeed, for Temple Shalom members, as well as for many other American Jews, the prophetic tradition acts as a powerful agent, justifying an ethic of social justice and political involvement.

The identification of Judaism with liberalism has American, as well as European, roots. The Reform movement's embrace of liberalism as its guiding ideology reflects its rise as a modernizing ideology, an ideology of accommodation to Western culture (Fishman 1974, 134–39). Accommodation to American patterns is evident, as well, for moralism, rather than pietism or theology, has been the mark of American religious life in general (Herberg 1960, 83–84; Blau 1976, 9–10, 18–19).

Given these influences, it is not surprising to find at Temple Shalom the type of Jewish ideology which prevails. The tenuousness of such a definition of Judaism, however, presents problems for some individuals, those who have the need or desire to identify the specifically Judaic component of their Temple's ideology. It is clear that most members are not Jewishly literate; that is, they are not well versed in Jewish history, texts, or thought. Confronted with situations in which they are called on to articulate the basic nature of Judaism or to explain the symbolic significance of certain ritual symbols, they frequently rely on an expert to do the job. They feel ideologically incompetent.

Fein et al. reveal similar observations in their study of Reform synagogues. They write:

> This ideological crisis is not, in the first instance, a question for theologians or philosophers. What we find is that people with very potent Jewish instincts feel that they have no way of supporting those instincts intellectually. . . .This is a source of substantial personal distress, all the more so as it is extremely difficult to transmit instincts to the young when the justification for those instincts has been lost, or is uncertain. . . .
>
> Most adult Jews of this generation have rich enough a set of Jewish memories that they can act out of their Jewishness in a framework of memory and instinct, even where theory is wanting. For younger Jews, whose memories are less ample and whose instincts are most austere, the matter may be very difficult. (Fein et al. 1972, 142, 144)

Temple Shalom's ideology runs the risk of failing to ring true to the younger generation through its inability to express the meaning of its Judaism beyond an identification with liberalism or in contrast to the received tradition. That generation, not raised during the height of American liberalism, most likely fails to have the pseudoreligious associations toward the secular liberalism that informs Temple Shalom's ideology and the parents' consciousness. In the case of one such member of the new generation, a sense of estrangement from a more substantive and traditional Judaism led her to dichotomize her identity as a Jew and her identity as a Temple Shalom member.

As modern persons appear to suffer from the under-institutionalization of private life, so perhaps it can be argued that at Temple Shalom people are ideologically underinformed. This may be precisely the reason why many people belong to Temple Shalom, that is, because they do not have to modify their existing ideologies or become Jewishly knowledgeable. The price that is paid, however, is a tenuous Jewish identity as far as a cogent philosophical posture is concerned. The transmission of the substance of such an ideology to future generations—a constituent element of Jewish continuity and survival—becomes the problematic challenge of such a position.

FOUR _____

Ritual and Identity

One of the contributions of secularization to modern society has been the devaluation of ritual. Moderns have generally experienced a loss of ritual awareness and, in fact, generally assume that ritual is useless (Sullivan 1975, 10).[1] Undoubtedly, this assumption reflects the rationalistic and perhaps unimaginative mentality of moderns, that is, the commitment to empiricism and science that limits inquiry to observable phenomena and distrusts activities that appear "magical."

Worship, the major manifestation of institutionalized religious ritual in the West, assumes the dialogue between the individual and God, the confrontation of persons with the transcendent Other, with the *mysterium tremendum* (Otto 1958, 12).

For moderns in general, and for contemporary Jews specifically, the experience of worship is a difficult one, since the reality of God is an uncertain proposition. (We saw this in Chapter Three.) The main goal of prayer for Jews today seems to be, not communication with God, but rather study, meditation, or the rediscovery of community and individuality: "Prayer is still the pretext, but the justification of the act, the real purpose, is now achievement of community, the sense of belonging" (Hoffman 1975, 48).

Worship is considered to be a principal activity of the synagogue. In studying the ritual life of Temple Shalom, Monica Wilson's insight regarding the nature of ritual is instructive:

> Rituals reveal values at their deepest level. . . . Surely men express in ritual what moves them most, and since the form of expression is conventionalized and obligatory, it is the values of the group which are revealed. I see in the study of rituals the key to an understanding of the essential constitution of human societies. (1954, 240)

More specifically, Hoffman posits that in the liturgical message, which

65

includes everything from the meaning of prayers to the music of the choir, "lies the key to Jewish identity" (Hoffman 1977, 131).

These views suggest that ritual expresses patterns of meanings held by a community, but that it also has a role in the construction of the community's world view and ethos, its view of reality and its values. Beyond this, however, rituals express patterns of social relations, as Durkheim (1965) argued in *The Elementary Forms of the Religious Life*. The study of ritual life at Temple Shalom is thus seen as a vehicle for understanding the institution's values, self-definitions, social relations, and mechanisms for structuring Jewish identity.

If modern Jews, like other moderns, have difficulty with religious ritual and with worship, one can readily assume that their involvement in these activities is complex and ambivalent. In effect, the ritual life of Temple Shalom reflects certain major themes, all fraught with tension and ambivalence, tensions between modernity and tradition, universalism and particularism, hierarchy and egalitarianism, formality and spontaneity, individualism and community, and intellect and emotion. The ritual life of Temple Shalom thus reveals the construction of a Jewish identity that is complex, ambivalent, and precarious. The picture that emerges is consistent with the portrait of the ideological dimension.

The Ritual Context

The sanctuary is the site of Temple Shalom's ritual life. It is a large and stately hall separated into two unequal portions. The bima is the raised platform area in the front part of the sanctuary, connected to the larger, lower area by five steps. The lower area contains rows of congregational pews, divided into three sections by two aisles.

The bima contains all the ritual and symbolic objects of the sanctuary: the ark with its Torah scrolls; a large, floor-sized, seven-armed candelabrum (menora); and the eternal light *(ner tamid)* in the shape of the traditional priestly symbol of hands extended in blessing. Several chairs are placed along two walls of the bima; these are used by the clergy and by a member of the board of trustees—frequently the president—during services. Portable chairs accommodate the choir on the bima, as well.

In addition to the symbolic objects on the bima, a set of small stained-glass windows of an abstract design is located on one wall of the sanctuary. The rest of the light stucco walls remains unadorned. The sanctuary as a whole is designed to reflect the colors of the tabernacle prescribed in the Torah (Exod. 25:4), hence blue, purple, and red figure prominently in the furnishings and carpeting of the sanctuary. The wood so generously used for chairs, pews, lectern, and ark doors likewise reflects the call for acacia wood in the Bible (Exod. 25:5). It may be recalled that the building as a whole, when viewed from outside, is designed to effect the shape of the tent of meeting. The symbolism used in this fashion is therefore self-consciously biblical. However, on the whole, the sanctuary looks starkly elegant and somewhat more Scandinavian in design and style than highly Jewish in symbolism.

One of the rabbis suggests that the abstract architecture of the sanctuary lacks specific Jewish symbols, such as Hebrew letters or a star of David. This, in his opinion, combined with the absence of ritual garb during services, results in a kind of symbolic sterility. He reports to have heard comments and criticisms about the Temple not showing more tangible symbols of Judaism. But he is also aware that a significant portion of the congreation has a "highly attenuated sense of Jewish identity and relationship to the synagogue." Therefore, he feels that through its symbols and words Temple Shalom expresses a specific kind of Jewishness:

> It is a Jewishness that is in touch with modernity and with the issues of modernity. It is a Jewishness, as articulated by the rabbis, that makes no pretenses to total knowledge and is aware of—doesn't celebrate but is aware of and accepts as a given—a sense of alienation from the categories of the Jewish tradition. [This Jewishness] is shared by the rabbis.

This attenuated Jewishness is expressed, then, through restrained Jewish symbolism and an abundance of aesthetic sophistication. But these two characteristics cannot be rigidly polarized because the religious symbolism that exists is unmistakably Jewish. Biblical association are undoubtedly intentional, expressing perhaps greater comfort in association with ancient Judaism than with its more recent expressions. As one of the rabbis opines:

> The most immediate predecessor of the synagogue is that of the social structures of Eastern European Jewry, most of which are not

particularly desirable as models: They were hierarchical, autocratic, nondemocratic institutions. . .and the synagogue was an expression and a bastion of it. . .like the Church in medieval times.

At Temple Shalom, association with Jewish symbolism is therefore selective. As this rabbi adds:

This congregation could not have a star of David in the sanctuary. This is too "hokey" a symbol. It comes to mean an uninterrupted continuity with the time of David, and people don't identify with this.

Nonetheless the synagogue uses a very ancient and certainly traditional symbol in depicting the eternal light in the form of a priestly blessing. The symbolic selectivity, as well as the choice of few rather than numerous Jewish associations, shows a self-identity that wishes to be cosmopolitan and aesthetically sophisticated, yet at the same time expresses an identification with the religious roots of Judaism, based on biblical rather than on more recent Jewish identifications.

The Sabbath Service

The Prayerbook

Shabbat (the Sabbath) is celebrated on Friday nights at Temple Shalom. Prayerbooks, selected beforehand by the clergy, are handed out by ushers at the entrance to the sanctuary. One of several prayerbooks is used: the old or new Reform prayerbooks (*Union Prayer Book* 1956 and *Gates of Prayer* 1975, respectively) or one of the prayerbooks compiled by the clergy and congregants. The most frequently used prayerbook is from the latter category. A brief examination of the liturgical message implicit in this prayerbook provides some insight as to the Jewish identity of Temple Shalom. As Hoffman argues:

Once the people begin using the [prayer] book. . .the book's message acts as a socializing agent to heighten the ideal image it represents. . .once accepted. . .the prayerbook message. . .becomes an active ingredient in forming group identity. (Hoffman 1977, 146)

Perhaps a minor but nonetheless symbolic message expressed by this prayerbook resides in the fact that the book opens from left to right, as opposed to the traditional prayerbook which, written in Hebrew, opens from right to left. Temple Shalom has chosen to contemporize the liturgical experience in this way, expressing thereby an identification away from the tradition and in favor of a modern, American option (for a related discussion, see Hoffman 1977, 144).[2]

In contrast to the traditional prayerbook—or even Reform's *Union Prayer Book* (1956) or *Gates of Prayer* (1975)—the prayerbook compiled by Temple Shalom has little Hebrew in it. While major blessings and a few principal prayers do appear in Hebrew, they are frequently transliterated into Latin script for the use of non-Hebrew readers. Some of the Hebrew portions are translated into English. Very often, however, Hebrew sections are accompanied, not by translations, but by alternative English readings; in this case the English selection, and not the Hebrew, is generally read. One clear message that emerges from this is that the congregation is not traditionally grounded and most people do not know Hebrew. By offering a creative English adaptation of traditional Hebrew prayers, the prayerbook, in effect, translates freely from one world view to another: from tradition to modernity. An example will serve to explain this dynamic.

The Shema, considered the central statement of faith in the unity of God, is surrounded by blessings before and after it. The second blessing preceding the Shema in Temple Shalom's prayerbook is presented in Hebrew, and then an alternative English selection is offered. Presented here for the sake of comparison, a literal translation of the Hebrew is followed by the English reading. It should be kept in mind that the Hebrew of this particular blessing is seldom read, while the English version is. Also, most congregants do not read or understand Hebrew, so even if the Hebrew version were read publicly, or if the individual were interested in reading the original silently, in most cases the meaning would not be accessible. In short, the traditional world view is in this way rendered unavailable to the congregation. A literal translation looks like this:

> Thou hast loved the house of Israel with everlasting love; thou hast taught us Torah and precepts, laws and judgements. Therefore, Lord our God, when we lie down and when we rise up we will speak of thy laws, and rejoice in the words of thy Torah and thy precepts for evermore. Indeed, they are our life and the length of our days; we will meditate on them day and night. Mayest thou never take away thy love from us. Blessed art thou, O Lord, who lovest thy

people Israel. (*Daily Prayer Book* 1949, 258)

Temple Shalom's version reads as follows:

> Once we knew one truth, and it was cherished or discarded, but it was one, and keeping or losing it we felt secure. Now we know the world can be interpreted by many truths, and the facts all perceive can be explained by truths some deny.
>
> Once we knew one kind of life, one morality, and it, too, we adopted or we scorned, but right was clear and wrong was always wrong. Now we know that there are many rights, and what is wrong may well be what is wrong for you, but right for me.
>
> Yet we sense that some acts must be wrong for everyone, and that beyond the many half-truths must be a single Truth all humanity may one day grasp. That clear way, that single truth is what we seek to glimpse in coming here, to join our people who saw One, where others could see merely Now. One truth behind the many truths, one way behind the many ways, one world encompassing them all.

The literal translation clearly stresses the legalistic aspect of the tradition, that is, the observance of precepts and laws thought to be central in the covenant between God and Israel. The reference to Israel at the beginning and end of the blessing stresses the particularism of the relationship involved, the specialness of the Jewish people.

Temple Shalom's version is not completely disassociated from the original; it could be suggested that the new reading is, in fact, in dialogue with the original, since the unity in truth, life style, and morality that it almost nostalgically recalls refers precisely to the "Torah and precepts, laws and judgements" mentioned in the original. But the new version is a clear recognition of the pluralism and relativism of the modern world; and although it suggests "that single truth is what we seek to glimpse in coming here," at no point does it concretely suggest the traditional option as a way for these Jews to seek this single truth. The absence of reference to Israel or the Jewish people, coupled with the hope for "a single Truth all humanity may one day grasp," reveals a universalistic commitment in contrast to the particularism of the original.

Another example from the prayerbook might help to uncover further values held by Temple Shalom. The traditional prayerbook has the following reading after the opening of the ark, immediately preceding the reading of the Torah:

> And it came to pass, whenever the ark started, Moses would say: "Arise, O Lord, and let thy enemies be scattered; let those who hate thee flee before thee." Truly, out of Zion shall come forth Torah, and the word of the Lord out of Jerusalem.
>
> Blessed be he who in holiness gave the Torah to his people Israel. (*Daily Prayer Book* 1949, 364)

At Temple Shalom this reading is omitted. Instead, the following statement, based on the Reform *Union Prayer Book* (1956, 94–95), is made by the rabbi after the Torah scroll is removed from the ark:

> This is the covenant that dedicates the Jewish people to the pursuit of justice and peace. This is the Torah, the pillar of right and truth. This is the law that proclaims that humanity is one, even as God is One.

By choosing to omit the traditional blessing and to offer this substitution, Temple Shalom once more selects a universalistic over a particularistic commitment. Whereas the original cites a number of specifically Jewish symbols—Moses, Zion, Jerusalem, "his people Israel"—Temple Shalom translates the meaning of the covenant and Torah into a universalistic social ethic, one destined to proclaim "humanity is one even as God is One." The prophetic nature of this declaration stems from the Reform heritage, as has been seen. However, it is interesting that a cursory examination of similar blessings in the two standard Reform prayerbooks shows a closer alliance of these with the traditional statement than does Temple Shalom's (see, for example, *Union Prayer Book* 1956, 94–95; *Gates of Prayer* 1975, 417–18, 425, 431–32, 437, 443).

So far, we have seen areas of discontinuity with the tradition reflected in the prayerbook. A connection with the tradition is also discerned, however. The basic structural elements and order of the traditional service are retained, although often in a considerably abbreviated version. Some of these key elements of the traditional liturgy appear and are recited in Hebrew, with transliterations and literal translations available; they are offered side by side with the more contemporary visions of reality expressed by many of the readings.

For example, the traditional blessings over the lighting of the Sabbath candles, recited at the beginning of services at Temple Shalom, reads, "Blessed art Thou, O Lord our God, King of the universe, who hast sanctified us by Thy laws and commanded us to kindle the Sabbath lights." It is a fact that members of Temple Shalom observe neither the Sabbath, in its prescribed fashion, nor the other commanded laws. But the maintenance of the liturgical order provides Jews with a sense of linkage to their past, while the recitation of traditional prayers makes the past a part of their existence. At the same time, these prayers give Jews a sense of continuity with Jews of other places (Kravitz n.d., 5). In addition, songs during services are almost unexceptionally sung in Hebrew, with the use of transliterations. It may therefore be suggested that the use of Hebrew, in both song and prayer—like the retention of the liturgical order—serves as a link to a common tradition, one which allows Temple Shalom's congregants to feel part of an ongoing community. Despite profound ideological differentiation from the tradition, exemplified by the alternative readings in English, Temple Shalom chooses in these ways to remain attached to that tradition.

Beyond this, however, an entry into a kind of sacred dimension is facilitated by the use of Hebrew. Hebrew, the language of the traditional synagogue, is for American Jews, as it was for their ancestors, unrelated to their everyday language. Hebrew, as a special kind of communication, carries "the intimations of a transcendent reality—just because its sounds do not translate themselves. . . into any objective references to mundane existence" (Petuchowski 1972, 48).

However humanistic and prophetic the content of the service, therefore, Temple Shalom provides some mechanisms for entry into the sacred by persons who, in large measure, have become secularized in thought; this is effected by the retention of Hebrew in ritual celebrated by congregants who do not understand it. Additionally, Hebrew is the language of the Jewish people and hence provides for a particularistic dimension amidst the universalism of the manifest content of the service. For as we have seen, the liturgy in general reveals a concern with humanism, universalism, and modernity and the conviction that traditional answers are inadequate to the solution of modern dilemmas. Yet traditional formulae and Hebrew are retained because they furnish a common heritage and therefore help to forge a shared identity, however tenuous its content might be. It is this effort to achieve some kind of balance that Temple Shalom's cantor may have had in mind when he declared, "Regardless of how liberal we want to be, there still is the desire to link ourselves with the tradition."

The Normative Ritual

SPATIAL AND BEHAVIORAL MESSAGES. The Friday night Sabbath service, the principal ritual event, most directly bespeaks the values of Temple Shalom. Therefore, I refer to it as the "normative" ritual. A typical service begins at 8:30 P.M. The door to the sanctuary represents a kind of threshold between one kind of reality and another, perhaps not the conventional separation between the sacred and the profane, but one between "regions" (Goffman 1959, 106) or "finite provinces of meaning" (Schutz 1971, 231). Different comportments seem appropriate in these two regions. Whereas informality, casualness, and expression of emotion characterize the personal interactions in the lobby outside the sanctuary, decorum, formality, and behavioral choreography inform the feeling tone inside.

The beginning of the service represents a transition from one region to the other. The cantor, guitar in hand, stands below (on the level of the congregational pews as opposed to above, the bima) and leads the congregation in song. Designed to create a mood for worship, active congregational participation is encouraged and frequently achieved in the singing. The mood is still a fairly informal one, as the cantor teaches the Hebrew words and melody of several songs.

A firm entry into the second region is accomplished when the cantor ascends the steps to the bima, puts down his guitar, and takes his place at the lectern. The latter is, in fact, the center of ritual action: It is there that all ritual actions are initiated by the clergy, who stand facing the congregation. The rabbis lead the congregation in prayer by reading portions of the service and initiating responsive reading. They handle ritual objects, such as the Torah scroll and its accoutrements; give sermons; and, when appropriate, bless individuals. The cantor chants the Torah portion of the week and is in charge of the music. A composer of some renown, he and the choir frequently perform new musical arrangements of the traditional liturgy to the accompaniment of the organ.

A major characteristic of this service is that it constitutes what Ducey calls a "mass ritual," in which an audience "responds to the presentation of the sacred symbols as a unified body, a mass" (1977, 6). As specified above, the role of initiating action, utterance, or music is assigned to the clergy; the space is divided so that specific boundaries clearly separate a more sacred from a less sacred zone (ibid., 6–8)—the bima and below, respectively.

In contrast to the rather democratic, participatory singing prior to the formal start of the services, music during the service itself frequently is in the category of performance rather than a participatory experience. The cantor, the choir, and the organ in effect provide a very striking musical experience which people appreciate as observers or as audience.

The sermon plays a central role in the service; it is also an activity that is received rather than initiated by the laity, since very clearly it is the product of expert personnel.

Neither the clergy nor the great majority of the congregants wear ritual garb during services. There is also an absence of traditional ritual gestures, such as bowing or *shuckling* (swaying back and forth) during prayer. A traditional ritual procession, the circumambulation with the Torah, has been introduced in the last few years; however, the reaction is not uniformly positive, as we shall see.

The recent reappropriation of a traditional ritual gesture reveals some of the tensions evident in the ritual life of Temple Shalom. The traditional response to the Bar'chu, the prayer that signals the call to worship, involves the leader of the service facing the ark and bowing as a sign of reverence (the congregation does the same). Until the recent reappropriation of this ritual gesture by the cantor at Temple Shalom, the clergy who stood at the lectern at this point—the cantor and a rabbi—would simply continue to face the congregation while the prayer was recited, without turning or bowing. Once the cantor began the traditional practice, one of the rabbis followed suit: "I like it. When I saw _____ [the cantor] turn, I wasn't sure what to do, so I started to turn too. It is a rare moment of inwardness for me, of ark-centeredness." The choir and the president of the board—all on the bima—also embraced this new behavior.

The other rabbi, however, has continued to face the congregation during this time, seemingly unwilling to adopt this ritual gesture. This behavior is aesthetically jarring in a place so clearly committed to a polished and highly choreographed performance. The cantor and this rabbi seem to express, respectively, commitments to the traditional and the antitraditional. Ritual response—whether pro or con— appears, in this case, to supersede strictly aesthetic considerations.

The end of the service provides for a reentry into the more

informal region that prevails before the cantor's ascent to the bima. The cantor, playing the guitar, leads the congregation in an upbeat song. Congregants put their arms around each other and sway to and fro with the music. At the conclusion of the singing, there is general kissing, shaking of hands, and wishes for a "Good Shabbos." The clergy enter the downstairs portion of the sanctuary, at which point they also engage in warm and informal greetings with the congregants. The entire congregation then moves to the social hall for kiddush (blessing over wine) and Oneg Shabbat (celebration of the Sabbath). The latter signals a complete reentry into the mundane; a social hour ensues, with food and conversion as its main features.

A variety of value messages emerge from this brief description of the spatial and behavioral characteristics of the normative ritual. The separation between clergy and congregation along vertical planes, with the former "upstairs" in front, and the latter "downstairs," is of course not unique to Temple Shalom. Rather, it reflects the innovations of nineteenth-century Reform Judaism away from the tradition and in greater conformity with Western, Christian architectural style. The traditional synagogue's bima was at the center of the sanctuary, with seats around it. Although also elevated, its distance from the congregation was not as dramatic as the height of the present design, for as the Torah was read, it was visually accessible to greater numbers of people than the present arrangement affords.

Along with spatial modifications, the modern synagogue transferred leadership from the laity to the clergy. In the traditional synagogue, a lay person, or more often the *chazzan* (cantor), led services by serving as the reader of the congregation; his function was not to read *in place of the congregation*, but rather to set a tempo for congregational prayer, which was not recited in unison, but rather, with each person reading, mostly out loud, at his or her own pace. These factors made for a kind of democratic style, as Mihaly suggests:

> One wonders whether the democratic nature of the synogogue which found expression in the liturgy and in the very design of the structure has not been seriously impaired by the tendencies of the nineteenth and twentieth centuries.[3] (1958, 313)

Through its hierarchical structure, this mass ritual at Temple Shalom concentrates power in the hands of the clergy. The ritual locates authority in the clergy by virtue of their knowledge, ritual competence, and moral charisma. Their place "above" the congregation ratifies this view, by physically and visually setting apart the more sacred from the less sacred. Sacrality inheres in the clergy because of their closer proximity to the ritual objects; their moral authority is also constituted by their access to the meaning of the ritual objects and the ritual events. The congregation is largely unlearned in ritual and liturgical matters, and this, in itself, relegates leadership to a class of experts.

Whereas in traditional worship most congregants had access to the prayerbook and were familiar with the Torah and its rituals, at Temple Shalom—as in American Jewish life, in general—the clergy have become religious leaders by default. The rabbi's priestly role, that of conducting services, is a modern role, unnecessary in times when all worshippers participated actively in prayer.

Today, however, the service has become leader-oriented, leading to an attitude of passivity among the congregation: "The fact that the reader faced the congregation in prayer further aggravated the process" (Mihaly 1958, 313). Hence at Temple Shalom, as the clergy lead services, the congregation is passive much of the time; they respond when prompted, listen to rabbinic reading or sermonizing, or sit back and enjoy a musical performance.

Despite the attenuated participation of the congregation in the normative ritual, services are nonetheless imbued with a kind of functional sacrality, one that inheres in its styles of decorum. By making radical separations between appropriate behaviors in two finite provinces of meaning—that is, between worship and nonworship comportments—Temple Shalom succeeds in creating a mood that differs radically from ordinary time. This mood is in part created by highly polished transitions from one region to another, punctuating one with elegance, quietude, high performance, and stylization while permitting greater spontaneity, emotional expression, and ordinariness in the other. It is doubtful that these characterizations constitute the usual distinctions between sacred and profane, if one considers substantive characteristics of these dimensions. Yet taken at a functional level, the worship experience differs sufficiently from ordinary time to be considered "set apart" (Durkheim 1965).

PERSONAL RESPONSES. Between forty and one hundred members attend an average Shabbat service. Clearly this represents a small percentage of the membership at large. In this regard Temple Shalom is typical of other liberal synagogues, with special services, particularly the high holidays, drawing large numbers. The congregation at services is normally an almost exclusively adult one, except when there is a bar or bat mitzva. At these occasions many children are present, as are numerous guests, inflating the usual congregation to two or three hundred in number.

Members offer a variety of reasons for attending services. Some have acquired the custom of going to services on the Sabbath, feeling that "on Friday nights, one goes to Temple." Included in this group is a couple who proudly states that "we even went to services during our honeymoon!" Some individuals suggest that services provide rest and relaxation from the pressure and business of the week, bringing an end, therefore, to the workaday week. In this sense, the service acts to separate the mundane week from the more special—if not necessarily sacred—nature of weekend life.

Many people offer that it is really the sermon which attracts them to services. The president of the board of trustees, for example, feels that "most adults come to services, not to worship, but to hear the sermon." Congregants are proud of the articulateness and brilliance of the rabbis, and they often state that the sermon is the highlight of the service. One member says, "I like to hear the sermon. I must confess that I often come late to services, with no compunction whatsoever, to hear the sermon. . . . I may walk in half an hour late or so." The attraction of the sermon is related to its perceived high intellectual level and its ethical tone:

> The principal attraction that Temple Shalom has for me is the intellectual level of the sermons. I'm not an Orthodox Jew, in the sense that my religious satisfaction comes from ritual observance. Rather, my satisfaction comes out of the ethical and moral imperatives of the religion, particularly as they are brought out at a level that I am comfortable with.

On the other hand, there are those who feel that the sermon, as an expression of high-level intellectuality, is a hindrance to spiritual experience. One member has stopped attending services on a regular basis, which he used to do, because

> I got discouraged with ritual. . . . I just feel that the rabbis are not interested in ritual. Services don't give me what I need. I would

like more innovation in ritual, with a goal to increasing the
emotional experience and fulfillment. I'm beginning to feel that
the highly intellectual content of services is anathema to spirituality. . . .The sermon represents the spiritual deadness of Jews in
our society.

Another member, who does not worship regularly, suggests that
although she sometimes finds services satisfying, "I find that the
services have an insufficient emotional content. It is too cognitive.
I would like more singing, more of a feeling of welcoming Shabbat,
of joyousness."

While some people mention that services allow for a kind of comfort and security inherent in the regular repetition of ritual, the single
most central motive offered for service attendance is the experience
of community. Hence one member says, "Prayer is not so important
every evening I'm there. I am committed to community, the fact that
others may need me to be there." One member whose spiritual needs
are unfulfilled at Temple Shalom nevertheless says:

> We love the Temple. It is completely a part of our lives, and we get
> a lot out of it for our lives, so we stay anyway. It offers me a sense
> of community, of people and friends. But the Temple has less and
> less to do with religion for me and more to do with people. I have
> a private life when it comes to religion. . . .Yet I like the services
> for what they do give me: They are peaceful, they provide the sense
> of community, they provide the opportunity to be reminded of my
> heritage and my roots, which I like. I also like the ritual and
> repetition in my life, though at Temple it is not of a religious nature.
> I like reaffirming the sense of community, and to experience Jewish
> things.

An interesting omission in most respondents' comments is the
absence of a spiritual or religious calling as a source of motivation
in synagogue attendance. The following response is atypical because
of its reference to God:

> I believe in God, though I'm not sure what I mean by that,
> particularly since I very strongly believe in human self-determina-
> tion. Yet when I pray, particularly during the silent prayer, I
> definitely have my own prayer that I communicate, on a one to
> one, with Him (or Her), with a capital "H."

More characteristic, as was discussed in Chapter Three, is the absence of God-language, including such references from the pulpit. When God is mentioned, even by the rabbis, the referent is usually the God of history—ancient history—and not a transcendent reality which potentially confronts people today.

Asked whether she felt to be in dialogue with God at any time during services, one member answered:

> No, I don't feel that I am praying to God. I don't even know if there is a God. I know there is a belief in God, one that helped to write a very large body of ethics. But, for me, being at services involves an experience of community and, perhaps more importantly, an individual, personal experience.

It is not surprising, therefore, that worship is a difficult matter for many congregants. Referring to the nontraditional nature of Jewishness at Temple Shalom, one of the rabbis said about himself and his colleague: "We are people who can say to [the congregation]— in the singular or the plural—'We have trouble praying, don't we?' And we mean it."

In general, then, the worship experience for most congregants at Temple Shalom reflects the general characterization of American Jewry offered by Hoffman (1975, 48). For, as he suggests, once God is no longer the end of prayer, that is, the principal addressee of the worship experience, the goal of prayer becomes study, meditation, or the rediscovery of community and individuality.

Responses to the decorous style of services are mixed, with people suggesting both attraction to and dissatisfaction with it. One member encapsulates this ambivalence when he says:

> I am bothered by the formality of the place. In a way, this is nice; it is orderly and quiet....I would not like to deal with ineptness. If things were run ineptly, tardily, poorly, it would be more than I would want to deal with. They are concerned to do things well, comfortably, tastefully....But sometimes it is extreme, more than you want or need. It is very much a performance.

Another member suggests that excellence is tremendously important to the rabbis: "They want to maintain 'quality control.'" Consequently, according to another person, the current president of the board of trustees is the first who has made announcements from the bima, since the rabbis were worried about someone not reading well from the pulpit.

A member who was brought up in a more traditional setting suggests that

> the aesthetics fit a Reform orientation. It is very orderly, very prophylactic. . . .with a kind of antiseptic formality, a rigidity here. The rabbis do not like things out of order. . . .There is a kind of paradox between their liberalism and their sense of orderliness, their formalism.

As suggested, the decorum of the service is often associated with a quality of performance, which is appreciated for its beauty and impressive delivery; it is criticized by some, however, for closing off possibilities for congregational participation. The cantor, for example, feels that during services he has to "struggle psychically to be as if in shul [Yiddish term for a traditional synagogue] . . . and not in front of an audience." In regard to the rabbis, one member says, "They are focused on performance, not religious experience. They are closed to the mystery."

One of the rabbis suggests that, while leading services during the high holidays, he feels worried about the sermon, the cues, looking at people, trying to remember names and faces. With all these things going on, "I am not into the ritual experience. I'm an officiant. I'm a performer." Beyond this, he suggests that Reform Judaism has some problems with ritual, namely, "self-consciousness and overintellectuality about what we do."

Responses to the music during services are characterized by an ambivalence similar to that displayed toward the ritual-as-performance. While acknowledging that he loves the music, a member nonetheless says, "I'd like the congregation to organize a choir. . . . More participation would enhance the service, as opposed to the performer quality now." And another adds, "I would like spontaneity to allow for inaccurate harmony. . . . Structure seems to work against emotional satisfaction."

Many members feel that the music is an outstanding facet of worship, and many agree that the cantor is a most gifted musician and composer. One of the rabbis suggests that the fact that the choir is hired is not a problem: "A musically sophisticated group in the congregation wants 'high performance' and would be more concerned with whether the tenor is off key. . .than whether the choir is hired or not." Yet contrary opinions also prevail among congregants. As one offers:

> The idea of a hired choir rubs me the wrong way. I just don't think that the choir is a particularly Jewish institution. . . . I am bothered by the fact that they are performers. But I enjoy the music in general.

This statement raises an important issue in the experience of the normative ritual, namely, the tension between universalism and particularism. Already touched upon in regard to the symbolism of the sanctuary and the liturgical message, this tension is perceived, as well, in the music of the service.

Temple Shalom's cantor, who was raised in an Orthodox environment, suggests that the world of music if typified by a universal outlook, one that is stressed at this synagogue. He believes that the tradition is manifested through a "tribal, clan impulse, an inward move, a 'withdrawing inside.' " By contrast, universalism involves "the freeing of the self of such bonds, the opening of the self creatively." Speaking about himself, the cantor said: "I have a Jewish heart, I feel for my brethren," but at other times, "I reach out. . .to all people. I have an openness to relating to non-Jews, to the human element."

In his work at Temple Shalom, he attempts to balance both worlds, but, in effect, this is a continuing struggle, one which he has yet to resolve. At times he has a concern about being "too Orthodox" for the people of the congregation, given their lack of traditionalism or liturgical knowledge. Hence, what he does in part is in response to the congregants. He feels that much of what he does musically with the liturgy is lost on the congregation, since they are not knowledgeable. Beyond the fact that most do not know Hebrew, he suggests that "they lack the awareness. They come to services in a vacuum, they come with nothing. . . .The culture of worship has left their lives." He finds frustrating the responsibility of engaging congregants in worship, of continually having to "bring them in."

The tensions between particularism and universalism reflected in the cantor's and some members' experiences with music are also revealed in people's responses to ritual symbols, in a manner reminiscent of the yarmulke discussion reported in Chapter Three. This issue is often expressed as a tension between the emotions unleashed by ritual symbols and an aesthetic sensitivity that acts as a kind of filter or censor. One member articulates this dynamic in this way: "Part of me likes symbols, but my aesthetic side does not like 'tacky symbols.' They have to be well put up."

When asked about the circumambulation with the Torah,[4] members expressed a variety of responses: enthusiastic, aesthetically appreciative, hostile, and intellectualistic. The following will serve as illustrations:

> I love it. I would love to march behind the Torah.

> I used to tear up when the Torah came around. . . . I would get rather emotional, but what I felt was a sense of pride, seeing all those people's good feelings, love, and affection.

> I call it "the trouping of the colors." Emotionally, I like it. I see a lot of beauty and a tie to the past in it, but it is really not my style. . . . It appears to be on the level of idolatry for me.[5] I was raised in a very liberal, ultra-Reform temple. I am not used to it, and I have a loyalty to Reform, to a pragmatic approach to religion and don't believe in "tradition-informed" just for the sake of "tradition-informed."

> There is a kind of "waltzing matilda" in the kissing of the Torah. . . . I find it idolatrous.

> I love to watch it but can't kiss it. I feel it's phoney somehow. Maybe in my mind it's so Christian, it's like kissing the ring, like idol-worship. I don't have a particularly emotional response to it, but, then again, I don't have a ritualistic bent.

The last statement raises another issue which emerges in some members' characterizations of traditional ritual, in general. When asked what is the meaning of tradition or traditionalism for them, a surprisingly large number of respondents referred to ritual practices, such as dietary laws, wearing ritual garments, and lighting candles. Of greater interest, however, is the fact that many members express a negative attitude toward the tradition so characterized because they find it "inauthentic":

> A lot of this is repugnant to me because it is inauthentic, meaningless (at least it seems that way to me). I knew a lot of people, and they seemed to do it out of a sense of obligation; they would even derogate their own actions. They did not do any of this out

of personal desire or comfort...so, in a sense, it was almost hypocritical.

Another member, who associated tradition with the practices of a nearby Conservative synagogue, said:

> I don't respond well to this. I like Saturday morning services at
> _____, particularly seeing the old men. What I don't like
> is all the hooplah of the young people; it looks inauthentic, like
> they've superimposed something on themselves, something from
> the past, that looks odd. By contrast, I love to see the old men
> who have the Jewish memories from their own lives, their own
> experiences.

For this individual, then, traditional ritual is authentic and positive if practiced by those who are old, European-born, and who, in some way, presumably have internalized those traditions. But for the young, and therefore the modern American, a new form needs to be created to express ritual practices. According to this view, the old contents no longer fit contemporary reality.

A very similar sentiment was communicated by one of the rabbis during a sermon. He very beautifully outlined the nature and value of the traditional dietary laws and the role they played in the lives of the Jews' ancestors, namely, that of separating sacred from profane, thereby sacralizing mundane life. Yet the sermon's finale strongly affirmed this ritual practice as an historical memory, while arguing that "we as moderns must find our own ways of sacralizing life." This conclusion a priori dismissed any possibility of adopting these traditional practices, by labeling them appropriate only to an age now past.

The imperatives of rationality, including those of logic and consistency, inform, as well, the consciousness of Temple Shalom in its ritual life. As we have seen, some people relate to ritual in an emotional way, without bringing rational criteria into their responses. Others, however, expect rationality to prevail at all times and thus to serve as a guide to the ritual process. Recognizing that ritual serves to meet spiritual and emotional needs in some ways, the rabbis nonetheless finally side with the rationalist perspective in their own ritual preferences. In a discussion about the Torah portion that is read every Sabbath, for example, the rabbis expressed the feeling that reading many of the portions entails a suspension of reason:

> The spiritual part of us permits the temporary suspension of the
> rational in an experience that has abiding value for our congrega-
> tion and ourselves. . . .We [the rabbis] just don't think about it. If
> we did, we'd feel conflicted.

At the same time, one of the rabbis stated:

> I could do away with reading much of the Torah. I feel like an
> automaton, expected to show reverence for it, to read this jibberish.
> I find no redeeming significance in many of the portions. . . .I can't
> understand why enlightened people would want to do this.

Some of the members present at this discussion urged the rabbis
to forego reading unappealing portions sometimes and to select,
instead, readings from the prophets or from secular sources. Other
congregants objected, however, to this potential departure from the
tradition. They argued for the value of historical continuity, for the
appreciation of the Jewish past, and for the tie to other Jews
experienced in the performance of similar rites. As one member asked,
"What does it serve modern man to delete the past? We don't cut out
part of the *Iliad* or the *Odyssey*." To which one of the rabbis replied,
"But we also don't kiss the *Iliad*, hold it, caress it! . . . Some people
have stopped coming because we have too much ritual—empty
ritual—without meaning: mumbo jumbo."
    Despite this rationalistic bias, however, traditional ritual practice
at Temple Shalom has been augmented in recent years, largely at the
initiative of the cantor, according to many people. So while holding
a very rationalistic orientation toward the Torah portions, ritual
practice has been retained and probably will continue for the
foreseeable future. For, in spite of their commitment to change and
to reasoned decisions, some members are beginning to question the
value of change, as such. They express the view that a facile dismissal
of the tradition may have contributed to the feeling of rootlessness
and meaninglessness they see themselves and their children experienc-
ing today.

The Chaverim Service
Ritual of Reversal

In the early seventies, a *chavura* (fellowship group) was started at Temple Shalom by an assistant rabbi who is no longer with the congregation. *Chavurot* are part of a movement in American Judaism designed to provide more meaningful Jewish experiences to people both within and outside institutional structures. Some chavurot took the shape of communal living arrangements, while others became study groups or worship communities (see, for example, Neusner 1972). Synagogues began to develop their own chavurot, designed to provide a more involved, less alienated experience for its members.

The Temple Shalom chavura, the Chaverim, was organized mainly around ritual events, including Saturday morning services, holiday celebrations, and rites of passage. In the recent past, however, its activities have been principally linked to a monthly Saturday morning service.

Attendance at this service is rather stable, with fifteen to twenty-five members generally attending. Most of these members are also frequent attendants at the normative ritual. The significance of this service for this study inheres in its radical distinctiveness from the normative Friday night ritual, which has been referred to as a mass ritual. By contrast, this is an "interaction ritual" (Ducey 1977, 6–8), one typified by participation, egalitarianism, and informality.[6] Because it so radically reverses the usual characteristics of the normative ritual, I refer to this service as a "ritual of reversal."

The prayerbook that is used generally is not significantly different from the one used on Friday nights in terms of its liturgical message, but much of the service actually inverts the normative order of the mass ritual. The smaller size, in the first place, is an indication of a different social configuration. A major departure from the normative ritual is the location of the entire congregation on the bima itself. There is therefore no physical separation between those leading the service and those who constitute the congregation. A circular seating arrangement is formed by using portable chairs and by some people sitting down on the bima's floor.

The tone of the service is informal, with people dressed in jeans and other comfortable clothing (as opposed to dresses and jackets/ties on Friday nights). Services never seem to start on time, sometimes because a minyan—a quorum of ten—is needed but, more usually, simply because the ethos is one of leisure and casualness. At some point, there is a consensus that the service should begin.

Leadership is rotated among members. Leadership roles are selected from one service to the next, or they are assigned during the interim between services. In addition to the roles of service leader (the role occupied by the rabbis in the normative ritual) and cantor, different individuals are responsible for the Torah reading and for conducting a Torah discussion.

While very few children attend Friday night services, for the Chaverim service whole families attend. Children are frequently involved in the ritual, particularly in the handling of ritual objects; for example, they often help to "undress" and "dress" the Torah scroll. In the normative service, women play almost no role, except for the honor of lighting the Sabbath candles and, on very rare occasions, being called up for the Torah blessings (aliya). Women, however, often have key roles in the Chaverim service. Clerical attendance at this service is optional. When the rabbis do attend, they form part of the congregation but play no leadership role. When the cantor attends, he does not read the Torah portion, but he usually does lead the group in song. The context, plus his use of a guitar during the service, makes this function seem a more participatory experience than one of performance.

Because leadership roles change from service to service, authority is diffused rather than concentrated or identified with specific individuals. A sense of equality and sharing is the norm, with people participating with more involvement and gusto than is typical at the mass ritual. Very often portions of the service ordinarily read by a single reader (i.e., the rabbi) on Friday night are read in sequence or in unison by the congregants. Informality governs the conduct of the service itself. The leader on one occasion, for example, said, "Let's read the English now, together," in what appeared to be a spontaneous decision, in contrast to the highly professional rendition of the Friday night ritual.

The informality of attire and comportment seems to facilitate an emotional openness, as well, with people more readily expressive of their feelings. A vehicle for emotional and intellectual disclosure is provided by the Torah discussion period, where people feel free to react to the Torah reading with personal thoughts and feelings. This kind of openness is manifested also in ritual experimentation of various kinds. People who never wear ritual vestments on Friday night, for example, choose to do so here. This includes the cantor and one of the rabbis who often attends. It is not uncommon to see some participants shuckling or involved in other traditional ritual gestures not seen in the normative ritual. People also are willing to experiment with worship styles, including *davening* (chanting out loud, in non/unison style), when a leader chooses to teach them before the start of the service.

Asked why they attend Chaverim services, members stressed the value of participation in this ritual, as opposed to the experience of forming part of an audience during the normative ritual. Many associated feelings of warmth, humanity, and autonomy with participation in the manner of the ritual of reversal. A spiritual dimension was experienced by many, as well. As one member who attends both kinds of ritual responded:

> I come to the Chaverim service in order to be on the bima, close to the ark and the Torah...to share and participate as a group. I tend to see Temple Shalom as a kind of "home," and it's nice to be able to come here at a time when people are inclined to worship, which is not always the case during Friday nights. It is often possible to worship during the Chaverim service...sometimes it's even reverent.

The Chaverim service is seen as a shared worship experience by many of its participants. Torah discussions often reflect the modern mentality, insofar as some people have trouble entering the symbolic reality of the Bible. Yet, in form and style, the service rejects the major characteristics of the normative ritual: its formality, attenuated ritual symbolism, and expert leadership. The group, rather than specific individuals, becomes the seat of knowledge and of moral authority.

Analysis

It should be clear by now that ritual life at Temple Shalom reveals a variety of value tensions, what may otherwise be called ambivalence. Much of this tension arises because ritual—perhaps more so than any other symbolic form—involves a profound confrontation with the past, with the tradition of another time and place. Given the complex relationship that moderns have with the past and its values, it is finally unsurprising that ritual should articulate experienced ambivalence.

Like other modern religious institutions, Temple Shalom is caught between a commitment to modernism, universalism, and cosmopolitanism and a desire for particularistic community. Hence, it shows selectivity and ambivalence in various facets of its ritual life, whether one investigates its ritual symbolism, prayerbook, normative ritual, or its ritual of reversal. The Chaverim service highlights some of the basic value tensions evident in the synagogue and is therefore a useful tool in interpreting the nature of the normative ritual, as well.

According to O'Dea:

> An institutional complex may be viewed as the concrete embodiment of a cultural theme in the ongoing life of a society, as the "reduction" of a set of attitudes and orientations to the expected and regularized behavior of men. (1970, 243)

The normative ritual in good measure expresses the style and convictions of classical Reform, a movement that evolved in self-conscious support of modernity and its characteristics. It may therefore be argued that this ritual manifests the cultural themes of modernity or, otherwise put, that it resolves the synagogue's ritual ambivalence in favor of the values of modernity. This is not to say that the ambivalence is permanently or decidedly resolved, since it is clear that tradition informs some elements of ritual life. Nonetheless, the normative ritual publicly reflects messages that side with modern values. These conclusions are based on several considerations, among these the sparcity of particularistic symbols in the sanctuary and the universalism of the liturgical message expressed in the prayerbook; both of these have already been discussed. Additional modern emphases can be found in the Friday night Sabbath service.

The professionalism of the clergy, in part expressed by their sole leadership of the mass ritual, reflects modern specialization and differentiation, whose emergence was due partly to the division of labor. Emancipation and Americanization led to the "Protestantization of rabbinic functions" (Carlin and Mendlovitz 1975, 186), whereby some of the major functions of the Protestant ministry were incorporated into rabbinic responsibilities. Given the progressive loss of learning by the laity, a major function of the rabbi has become that of leader of worship services, a responsibility that, as we have seen, previously had rested in the hands of any Jew who was competent and acceptable to the congregation. The expectation that a specialist must lead services, reinforced by the lack of training in this area on the part of congregants, has contributed to the creation of a passive audience which listens and responds only to the promptings of the leaders.

This development in role specialization certainly contributes to the formal nature of the normative ritual. As Mary Douglas writes:

> It seems not too bold to suggest that where role structure is strongly defined, formal behaviour will be valued. . . . Formality signifies social distance, well-defined, public, insulated roles. Informality is appropriate to role confusion, familiarity, intimacy. (1973, 99–100)

Undoubtedly the formality of this ritual is also related to the "ordeal of civility" (Cuddihy, 1974) that Jews experienced in their movement toward modernization, emancipation, and assimilation. As Cuddihy suggests, the embrace of civility—the Western social aesthetic—was, for Jews, a major ticket of acceptance into modern society. Decorum and civility, both amply evident during Temple Shalom's normative ritual, are testimonies of the Reform movement's modernizing agenda. Their continued presence at the synagogue perhaps points to the ongoing commitment to that goal. As the Temple's handbook urges regarding "Temple Decorum," "during services, we are attentive and respectful."

The separation of the private sphere of life from the public is a characteristic of modernity that has been commonly observed. A consequence of such separation is the masking of personal feelings in public places, the development of what may be called "affective neutrality" (Parsons 1952, 59). Decorum necessitates the control of emotion for the sake of public presentation. One consequence of this dynamic is the presentation of a highly intellectualized experience at Temple Shalom, one which many find cold. Cuddihy writes, "To acquire the 'affective neutrality'. . .or 'emotional asceticism'. . .that civilizes one into modernity is to divest one's solidarity sentiments of their sacred particularity" (1974, 235). This insight might prove helpful in understanding the call for more emotional involvement issuing from some congregants; the need might be for greater particularity, as well as for greater emotionality.

Symbol systems have become increasingly universalistic as modernity has advanced and as the individual has become increasingly detached from group norms. Commitment to particularism, whether at the ideological, symbolic, or ritual level, has declined accordingly. Mary Douglas, for example, suggests that the move away from ritual is accompanied by a strong movement toward "greater ethical sensitivity" (1973, 41). In this light, the classical Reform movement's commitment to universalism and moralism expresses an essential move in the modernizing process. In embracing this perspective, the normative ritual reflects a modernizing tendency.

Especially interesting in this connection is the fact that many congregants find ritual expression to be inauthentic. According to Trilling (1972, 94), the concept of "authenticity" arose in the West only in the eighteenth century, once the individual's autonomy from society was becoming an expressed cultural goal. To see ritual behavior as inauthentic, then, is to interpret its enactment as a cultural invasion of the self. The self is seen as masquerading, expressing meanings that it does not believe in or understand, but which it expresses due to the coercive pressure of tradition. Hence, many congregants are suspect of people who are ritually observant, for clearly these people are seen as modern Americans involved in practices that belong to a different cultural epoch. This assumption calls forth expectations of modern commitments to individualism and personal, rather than cultural, expression. The inconsistency between this expectation and observed ritual behavior or certain types of symbolism is resolved by calling these "inauthentic," that is, not quite personally truthful.

The commitment to individualism is expressed in other ways during the normative ritual. As we have seen, ritual garments are optional, at least at a manifest level, allowing for personal predilection in this respect. Many of the creative readings in the prayerbook also reveal individualistic and private concerns.

In Chapter One, I discussed the fading of the past as the locus of value and authority for modern persons. One manifestation of such a phenomenon is the neutral or negative response to ritual symbols that some people seem to experience. Most impressively, this is the case with the rabbis' reaction to the Torah and the portions to be read from it during Sabbath services. In a sense, the Torah has become disenchanted for the rabbis. Its power has faded. Its sacrality is open to question. It no longer holds the mystery and awe that it did in times long past. It has been submitted to rational critique and has been found wanting. Yet the rabbis themselves admit that they are still drawn to it by their spiritual selves, those parts of themselves not operating under the law of reason.

Symbols of religious particularism have become opaque for many moderns; they no longer contain sacred meaning. Paul Tillich believed that when a myth is understood to be a myth, but not eliminated for that reason, it can be called a "broken myth" (1958, 50). Perhaps one can use similar language in regard to ritual symbols, such as the Torah, which no longer fire the religious imagination: They have become "broken symbols." The circumambulation with the Torah and the yarmulke are other examples that fit this categorization at Temple Shalom. They are broken symbols for some members and the clergy of this institution. Some of these broken symbols are maintained, however, in spite of the fact that they do not trigger much of a response from many people. Given the paucity of shared symbols, they may be retained because they help to furnish some of the commonality essential to community, particularly since many members attend services precisely in search of community. Writing about Reform Judaism, Bell offers an insight into this dilemma that supports Cuddihy's contention:

> The ethical view is fundamentally syncretistic, drawing from all faiths, for to be valid, an ethical precept must be binding on every man and applicable to all men....The ethical dissolves the parochial, and takes away from individuals that need for the *particular* identification which singles them out and shapes their community in distinctive terms: terms which make possible a special sense of belonging to the group. (Bell 1969, 468; emphasis added)

Particularism, in this view, is an essential ingredient of community; the latter cannot be sustained through a universal ethical ideology alone. Of course, Durkheim (1965) went even further when he argued that group solidarity is maintained only when particular ritual action reinforces belief.

The Chaverim service most specifically particularizes the ritual experience at Temple Shalom. It draws on some of the more traditionally oriented members of the congregation, but it also serves as a model of particularistic symbols and antinormative ritual form for people in search of community. The richness of this ritual experience provides members with a shared symbolism drawn from the Jewish tradition.

By contesting so many of the marks of modernity expressed in the normative ritual, the Chaverim service actually reflects sentiments that are kept in check or lie latent during the mass ritual. In spite of some people's dissatisfactions with the latter, as has been noted, the normative ritual is perpetuated. Channels for change do not appear to be readily available to many members of the congregation. One of the rabbis feels that by attending the Chaverim service he can "get out of the role of performer" and become a participant like others. Recall the cantor's concern that he did not want to appear "too Orthodox" to the congregation. This illustrates that even the clergy feel constrained to maintain the ritual status quo at the normative ritual, since they assume that large numbers of congregants expect that kind of format.

Some members of Temple Shalom desire greater informality, more emotionality, and greater participation in the normative ritual. The Chaverim service, in effect, meets all these needs, averting in some way the need for a dramatic confrontation about their absence in the normative ritual. A consistent group of people has participated for years in the Chaverim service, testifying thereby to a desire for an alternative ritual expression from the one normally found. The highly intellectual presentation of ritual on Friday nights is converted into an emotionally more accessible experience. The use of more ritual symbols in closer proximity to those present makes for a more direct encounter between the worshipper, ritual symbolism, and the traditional past. Likewise, the informality and general egalitarianism of the ritual allow for less separation between public and private experience. The presentation of self is not as highly stylized here, as participation largely replaces performance. All of these characteristics challenge the modernizing trends of the mass ritual. In these ways, the Chaverim service emerges as an expression of "demodernization," contesting such characteristics of modernity as alienation, bureaucratization, rationality, and affective neutrality implicit in the normative ritual (see Berger et al. 1974, 189–230).

Members who attend the Chaverim service and those who criticize the normative ritual for its failure to meet their needs for participation, emotionality, and spontaneity may be rejecting, in fact, the institutionalization of values and meanings which, expressive of a cultural theme of modernity, no longer meets their personal experience. According to O'Dea:

The process of objectification, which makes it possible for cult to be a genuine social and communal activity, can proceed so far that symbolic and ritual elements become cut off from the subjective experience of the participants. A system of religious liturgy may come to lose its resonance with the interior dispositions of the members of the religious body. In such a case the forms of worship become alienated from personal religiosity, and whereas previously cult had evoked and patterned response and molded personal religiosity after its own image, now such an overextension of objectification leads to routinization. (1970, 246))

Such an analysis may apply, as well, to those members who never attend services at all, and it may be expressive of the disinterest in worship seen among American Jews in general, particularly when contrasted to other Americans and their patterns of church attendance.

The Chaverim service must be seen in relationship to, rather than in isolation from, the normative ritual at Temple Shalom. For, in inverting dress, decorum, aesthetics, ritual symbolism, and leadership dynamics, this service is reacting to the normative order. Guided by Clifford Geertz (1973) and Victor Turner (1969), Babcock writes, "Such forms of symbolic inversion manipulate. . . and thereby question or dispute or at least comment upon the existing order of things" (1978, 26). She goes on to say that

All symbolic inversions define a culture's lineaments at the same time as they question the usefulness and the absoluteness of this ordering. . .they remind us of the arbitrary condition of imposing an order on our environment and experience, even while they enable us to see certain features of that order more clearly simply because they have turned inside out. (ibid., 29)

The normative ritual at Temple Shalom captures the commitment to a modern understanding of Judaism, one which uses some principal typifications of modern style, symbolism, and form. Expressive of early Reform's modernizing agenda, this ritual reveals the current members' proclivity for modern, universalistic styles of worship. But the relatively small attendance at services, the expression of criticism by regular members, and the presence of the Chaverim service are testimonies of a more complex and perhaps ambivalent constellation of values.

The Chaverim service should be seen within the larger context

of the chavura movement in American Judaism today. This movement is expressive precisely of the demodernizing or counter-
modernizing efforts of groups and societies of recent times that have
resisted the automatic assumptions and styles of the modern world
(see Berger et al. 1974, 189–230). The principal motivations that lead
people to join these organizations stem from dissatisfactions with the
normative synagogue fare. In rejecting the loneliness of a modern
society, including that found in the synagogue, people join chavurot
in quest of community. A recent study of chavurot suggests that
joining a chavura represents a move from actual passivity to the quest
for participation because, in modern life, virtually "all aspects of the
individual's life are mediated by one or another large organization"
and individual autonomy is "further blunted by the mystique of
specialization" (Reisman 1977, 38–39). Dependency on experts, likewise
a modern characteristic, leads to a quest for more authority. Finally,
recent developments in personal religiosity have meant that "more
and more people are unwilling to settle for a nominal religious
identification" (ibid., 53). People's struggles against meaninglessness
have led them to chavurot in pursuit of ideology, transcendence, and
meaning. (See Elazar and Monson 1979 for a recent study of synagogue
chavurot).

Temple Shalom's ritual of reversal may thus express a culturewide
phenomenon, namely, the rejection by some people of institutionalized
forms committed to modern cultural themes. Life-style experiments
and religious expressions of recent years (such as the turn to Eastern
religions, charismatic groups in Christianity, the chavura movement
in Judaism) are signs of cultural creativity, creativity that challenges
the objectification of institutional settings. The Chaverim service may
be expressive of precisely such a challenge:

> Such "creative negations" remind us of the need to reinvest the
> clean with the filthy, the rational with the animalistic, the
> ceremonial with the carnivalesque in order to maintain cultural
> vitality. (Babcock 1978, 32)

The Chaverim service is a statement that, for at least some
members, the normative order of ritual life at Temple Shalom does
not address their personal religious needs. It offers a model for injecting
creativity into ritual forms that no longer fire religious experience.
Ironically, the Chaverim service consists of a group of modern persons

who nonetheless reject some elements of modernity as they voluntarily select from a tradition whose focus is the past. In rejecting some of the values of modernity manifested in the normative ritual, this group uses forms from the tradition to meet current needs.

Uneasy companions, modernity and tradition thus appear to be inseparable elements in this synagogue's ritual life. For, after all, the congregants are modern persons who, by virtue of their affiliation with a religious institution, must deal somehow with their traditional legacy.

FIVE

COMMUNITY AND IDENTITY

"Community" is a rather imprecise term, insofar as it is used in various ways by different writers. Some use it as a synonym for society, social organization, or social system. Others employ it to denote biological or sociocultural concepts, such as an ethnic group or culture. Yet others stress subjective criteria, such as identification (Sjoberg 1964, 114–15).

In the present context, community is used, in the tradition of classical sociological theory, to denote a social group that provides integration, meaning, purpose, and moral cohesion to a social collectivity. Community in this sense constitutes moral community (Durkheim 1964). It furnishes personal identity by creating a sense of belonging, conferring status, and providing motivation for the individual. Through participation in community, therefore, the individual develops a sense of self (self-identity) and the perception of self by others (social identity). In community, also, an individual consciousness is acquired—an apprehension and interpretation of reality. In the final analysis, it may be argued that identity implies not only personal history but also social history (Strauss 1959, 164).

This is not to say that the individual is a tabula rasa upon whom social formulas are inscribed. Rather, the individual evolves in a dialectic with the communities to which he or she belongs or with those values he or she has embraced (his or her reference groups). The individual informs and shapes community, as he or she is informed and shaped by it (see Berger and Luckmann 1967).

Theologians interpret the individual's independence from, and consequent influence upon, collective meanings as the religious dimension in human experience. The inescapability of social nature is tempered by the individual's ability to transcend his or her communities in consciousness, to stand apart from the collectivity and evaluate it from the perspective of the "beyond," that is, with transcendent standards (R. Niebuhr 1955, 34–40; Tillich 1952, 86–154; Luckmann, though not a theologian, presents a similar argument in

1967, 41–49). Yet human givenness, with its psychological and social needs, motivates the individual, again and again, to seek community, to have the "courage to be as a part" (Tillich 1952, 89).

The problem of the modern age in regard to community is the atomization of individuals through the collapse of organic collectivities. Individualism, expressed in the philosophies of romanticism and existentialism, for example, has tended to view the individual person as fully autonomous, as a microcosm of the universe, without need of social ties (Tillich 1952, 113–54). The present so-called culture of narcissism (Lasch 1978) is a current expression of romanticism, in that its basic premise appears to be individual self-reliance and independence from social and public concerns. The rationalist image of humanity, emergent during the eighteenth and nineteenth centuries but still influential today, also assumed that individual freedom lay in emancipation from, rather than within, association (Nisbet 1953, 226).

Despite narcissistic inclinations evinced by many people in the current period, the growth of conservative churches and cultic movements in recent years can be seen as a reaction to the under-institutionalization of personal life. They have served as antidotes to personal alienation, alienation resulting from the loss of meaning, structure, and identity that community provides (see, for example, Kelley 1972; Klapp 1969).

The rise of fellowship groups (chavurot) among Jews in the last fifteen years also reflects unfulfilled community needs in the existing Jewish organizational structures. In a recent study of the Reform movement, the authors offer the following assessment:

> Through all our work, no single conclusion registers so strongly as our sense that there is, among the people we have come to know, a powerful, perhaps even desperate, longing for community, a long-ing that is, apparently, not adequately addressed by any of the relevant institutions in most people's lives. (Fein et al. 1972, 140)

Members of modern society, Jews also experience the loss of organic ties that once connected the individual to the group. Community, no longer based on mechanical solidarity, is today largely a result of voluntary association. Just as personal identity in a general sense involves the active participation of the individual in its design and direction, so Jewish identity, within the ambit of an institution, evolves through the process of deliberate construction and maintenance.

The Construction of Community Uniqueness and Identity

According to Martin Buber (1950):

> Community—not the primitive sort, but the sort possible and appropriate to modern man—declares itself primarily in the common and active management of what it has in common, and without this it cannot exist. . . .
>
> The real essence of community is to be found in the fact— manifest or otherwise—that it has a centre. The real beginning of a community is when its members have a common relation to the centre overriding all other relations. (Buber 1950, 133, 135)

In other words, a source of commonality is essential to the construction and maintenance of community. Commonality, in turn, is constituted by meanings and symbols shared by the group's members. Previous chapters have shown that Temple Shalom's ideology and ritual present the congregants with ambivalent and complex messages regarding the meaning of Judaism. In part, this is because of the precariousness of Jewish identity and meaning in the modern age, the lack of certitude and ambiguity regarding what it means to be Jewish and how it is desirable to be Jewish in a pluralistic, open society.

One source of commonality at Temple Shalom, then, is of a negative rather than a positive sort, namely, a shared ambivalence about Jewish identity, an ambivalence informed by both tradition and modernity. A clearer and more active source of commonality is the synagogue's elaboration of its identity around the mechanism of uniqueness. A functional rather than substantive or ideological mechanism, the "cult of uniqueness" serves to cultivate community and to promote commitment at Temple Shalom.

Temple Shalom develops and sustains a preoccupation with its own uniqueness as a way to create an image of itself that guarantees its members' allegiance. In doing so, Temple Shalom emerges with a distinct and highly defined image, making it thereby easier for its members to affirm their loyalty to it rather than to explore possible alternatives. As Kanter suggests:

> This process contains the first principles of a "gestalt sociology":
> to develop maximum commitment in its members, a group must
> form a unity or a whole, coherent and sharply differentiated from
> its environment—a figure clearly distinguished from the ground,
> whether the ground is the outside society or excluded options for
> behavior. . . .The group builds commitment to the extent that it
> clearly cuts off other possible objects of commitment, becomes an
> integrated unity tying together all aspects of life within its borders,
> develops its own uniqueness and specialness, and becomes capable,
> by itself, of continuing the person's gratification. The strength of
> commitment, then, depends on the extent to which groups institute
> processes that increase the unity, coherence, and possible gratifica-
> tion of the group itself, at the same time that they reduce the value
> of other possibilities. (Kanter 1972, 71)

This is precisely the role that the cult of uniqueness plays at
Temple Shalom.

The Temple Shalom Family

Temple Shalom frequently refers to itself as the "Temple Shalom
family," a designation felt to be fitting for an institution where warmth
and caring predominate over impersonality and divisiveness, typifications assigned to other synagogues. The metaphor of family as the
Temple's self-image uses the powerful associations of kinship structure
to cement communal identity.

The rabbis, without a doubt, are seen to be the heads of the Temple
Shalom family. The family imagery is stretched by some to the point
of calling Temple Shalom the senior rabbi's "baby." While in private
meetings or interviews members reveal some ambivalence toward the
rabbis, they also evaluate them in lavish and even superlative terms.[1]
A fairly typical perception of the rabbis is expressed by a member who
states, "I don't know very many rabbis, but I believe ours are better
leaders, better thinkers, brighter people." Other members provide more
explicit comparative perceptions when they argue that other rabbis
are pompous, inarticulate, and concerned solely with "money, numbers, and performance." By contrast, Temple Shalom's rabbis are
viewed as open-minded, in that they welcome freedom of expression
and disagreement from congregants; as superior speakers; as committed

to "the life of the mind." Unlike other rabbis, they are seen to be rebellious and to avoid trends and stultifying conformity; in a word, they are considered courageous. The superior quality of the rabbinic leadership is therefore seen to be a major contributor to the uniqueness of Temple Shalom.

The cantor is also viewed in a superior light. Appraised by one member as "one of the greatest Jewish musicians of the century," his music is considered far superior to that of other synagogues. Some congregants attribute their membership at the synagogue to the quality of the music, thus applauding the special abilities of the cantor, organist, and choir.

The membership itself is perceived to be unique and special. The "caliber of the people" is a frequent reason given for membership in the synagogue, even by those congregants who are dissatisfied with various facets of Temple life. The membership as a whole is seen to be intellectually impressive and personally warm and sociable. Many members' entire friendship circle is drawn from the Temple's membership.

A special source of pride to Temple Shalom is the fact that five rabbis are members of the congregation. Considered a note of distinction and an acknowledgment of Temple Shalom's uniqueness, this fact is frequently mentioned as a characteristic that differentiates this from other synagogues. As one of the rabbis suggests, "It's a feather in our cap to have a rabbi join."

All of the above characteristics serve to shape the uniqueness of the Temple Shalom family. Although the source of this uniqueness may be placed on the leadership or the specialness of the members, ultimately the institution as a whole is invested with charisma. Through this "institutionalized awe," a sense of transcendence is attributed to Temple Shalom; great power is seen to reside in the community, as such, and not only in its component parts (Kanter, 1972, 113).[2]

Differentiation from the Jewish Community

Developing an institutional identity involves drawing careful and specific boundaries that define the group, setting it off from its environment and giving it a sharp focus. Strong communities tend to have strong boundaries—physical, social, and behavioral. What goes on in the community is sharply differentiated from what goes on outside it. Beyond the differentiations that have already been mentioned in marking off Temple Shalom's identity from other synagogues, there are a variety of more specific mechanisms that elaborate on the cult of uniqueness. A number of such mechanisms serve specifically to separate Temple Shalom from the surrounding Jewish community, that is, from the institutions, ideology, and ritual that prevail in other Jewish organizations. Three particular differentiating mechanisms will be identified here: structural isolation, ideological differentiation, and ritual distinctiveness.

STRUCTURAL ISOLATION. Unlike other synagogues which are involved in joint programming with one another, Temple Shalom sees itself and is seen as a fairly isolated institution, staying aloof from Jewish communitywide programs and controversies. As one member puts it, "I don't think [the rabbis] care about that kind of involvement [with the larger Jewish community]. Temple Shalom traditionally has not been involved in the organized Jewish community." Another congregant interprets this orientation in this way:

> As a temple, it makes less of an effort to be part of the Jewish movement, except for social causes. If you think of yourself as unique, you'll be isolated. They go hand in hand. If you think of yourself as isolated, you'll be isolated.

In addition to abstention from interinstitutional gregariousness, Temple Shalom is differentiated from similar communities by the absence of a sisterhood or brotherhood within its structure. This fact isolates the Temple from membership in national sisterhood and brotherhood organizations, which would link it to encompassing community networks. A sisterhood and a brotherhood were in existence at Temple Shalom some years ago. It is unclear to people why they were dissolved. Some suggest that they were unsuccessful in maintaining themselves due to lack of interest. Others claim that the senior rabbi did not want them and hence disbanded them. Another opinion relates to the question of style or "fit": "The whole syndrome of sisterhoods...it's just not our own." Another way of saying this is to suggest that Temple Shalom is unique and different and that such usual congregational organizations are not appropriate for its sense of identity, that is, its self-image. A parallel situation is the absence of a gift shop here, another usual synagogal institution.

Temple Shalom's sense of being set apart from activities in the Jewish community is illustrated by the fact that, until recently, the congregation was not formally represented in a yearly communitywide march in support of the State of Israel. The Temple's religious school had been the only one in the area which had conducted classes on the day of march. When the synagogue decided to join the larger community in this show of Jewish solidarity, announcements regarding the march were made at meetings and mailed to members. Many members had not been aware of such a march until this point. The institutional insularity of the Temple is thus reflected in this sense of isolation experienced by the members.

IDEOLOGICAL DIFFERENTIATION. Although a gap exists between ideological rhetoric and practice at Temple Shalom (see Chapter Three), the synagogue nonetheless sees itself as actively holding commitments to social justice, social activism, and political liberalism. Members acknowledge that other synagogues also are involved in admirable social causes; they feel, however, that, in the present era of increasing political conservatism and self-interest that has penetrated the Jewish community, Temple Shalom remains a bastion of liberalism, with the rabbis as its spokespersons.

Unpopular in the eyes of the Jewish community at large, Temple Shalom has consistently taken radical positions vis-à-vis the Middle East, namely, a decidedly dovish point of view. In contrast to other segments of the organized Jewish community, the Temple has repeatedly supported affirmative action programs. Likewise, the rabbis have often spoken in support of school desegregation and in opposition to "white flight" into private schools. Members frequently speak with disdain of other synagogues in the area that have succumbed to that pressure.

In these ways, Temple Shalom sees itself as different from the normative Jewish community and therefore as unique and morally superior. Indeed, the senior rabbi believes that the function of Temple Shalom is to be "the pin in the ass of the community," a kind of modern-day Socratic gadfly. The Temple is therefore charged with the responsibility of acting as a moral force in the larger Jewish community in regard to issues of social and ethical moment. This task is probably seen as possible because of the independence of Temple Shalom from the Jewish community. Beyond this, however, is the assumption that Temple Shalom possesses the moral resources and perspective to carry out this responsibility.

Other treasured values are considered special marks of Temple Shalom, as well. The commitment to personal equality, typified by the absence of plaques and named funds, for example, is always offered as a sign of Temple Shalom's uniqueness, a quality perceived to be in sharp distinction to what is dominant in the Jewish community at large. As one member proudly declared, "We have no class system, no special seating, no differentiation of 'important persons.'"

The dues structure is seen as a fair and rather unusual one, in that it does not discriminate against those with limited incomes. Apart from the concern with justice implicit in this system, it also serves to give identity to the synagogue by differentiating it from the practices of most other synagogues. During a finance committee meeting, for example, when there were many problems balancing the synagogue's proposed budget, someone suggested the possibility of charging members for various activities that until then had been offered free of charge. Evidently distraught by this prospect, a participant quickly responded, "We are going to be just like every other temple, charging for everything we offer!"

Related to this commitment to egalitarianism is Temple Shalom's stance against the ostentatious show of wealth, seeing itself as set apart in this regard. At one time it seems that there was a prohibition against wearing furs to Temple. The rabbis have frequently talked to the congregants about the value of simplicity, specifically when decrying lavish displays at bar or bat mitzva extravaganzas found in other congregations.

Freedom of expression and respect for all points of view are considered unique features of Temple Shalom by many members. The rabbis are seen as the tone setters in this regard, but the congregation as a whole is viewed as one that is not trendy or conformist, one that upholds principles out of a sense of rightness rather than due to momentary pressures or idiosyncratic currents.

RITUAL DISTINCTIVENESS. In Chapter Four, the ritual life of Temple Shalom was examined, with attention focused on the ideological precepts that have informed it, most particularly the heritage of the classical Reform movement and other modernizing influences. It was suggested then that Temple Shalom has not adjusted to changes in the Reform movement that have tended to support increasing ritualism and the reappropriation of the tradition. A commitment to rationalism in part has been responsible for this reluctance to embrace ritual, seeing the latter as empty form rather than considered judgment. The commitment to individual freedom and personal choice has also been pitted against the presumed coercion of traditional ritual forms and garments. Finally, the ideological assumption that ceremonialism and social activism are antithetical has also dictated an antiritualistic orientation.

From a sociological perspective, however, Temple Shalom's reluctance to join the move of Reform Judaism to greater ritual expression and experience appears to constitute another mechanism for differentiation and hence identity construction. By remaining different in this area, the Temple is able to set strong boundaries and to establish a unique identity. An illustration of this argument is provided by a discussion emerging out of the yarmulke controversy (see Chapter Three). A congregant expressed great agitation during a ritual committee meeting, where the subject of making ritual vestments available for congregational use was being discussed. She was distressed about the possibility that

> Pretty soon one would walk into the sanctuary and find the rabbis wearing yarmulkes, wrapped in their *tallises* [prayer shawls], and so forth, and *we would be like any other synagogue, not like the Temple Shalom we have known and loved.* (emphasis added)

Style

Temple Shalom's style is considered by the congregation to be a fundamental source of specialness and distinctiveness. As such, it serves as an important mechanism in the cult of uniqueness and, therefore, of identity construction.

Style is a difficult concept to articulate. Most of what is known about style pertains to the fine arts, very little work having been done to date in discerning its role and significance in social contexts. Some transferability from the fine arts is perhaps possible, however, in illuminating the character and role that style plays in identity construction at Temple Shalom.

According to Kroeber, a style is

> a strand in a culture or civilization: a coherent, self-consistent way of expressing certain behavior or performing certain kinds of acts.

It is also a selective way: there must be alternative choices, though
actually they may never be elected. (1957, 150)

Hence, style is a form of communication, one chosen from among
alternative possibilities. But above all, what is most characteristic about
style is that form, the manner of expression, is more important than
content.

Three additional characteristics of style are pertinent here. First,
style refers to a unified expression, to a sufficiently consistent set of
forms that a coherent cultural gestalt is revealed, as opposed to
fragmentary group expressions (Schapiro 1953, 287).

Second, style is thought to be shaped by, and therefore expressive
of, "the 'inner form' of collective thinking and feeling" (ibid., 287).
That is, style reflects mentality or world view. Conversely, the Marxist
conviction that infrastructure determines suprastructure must be taken
into consideration. Hence, economic and political conditions, as
well as ideological factors, must be considered in the creation of a
group style.

Third, a style reflects intentionality, as well as expressivity; it has
normative, as well as descriptive, characteristics. It is this aspect of
style that is most relevant to the construction of identity, for apart
from expressing the broad outlook of the group, style "is also a vehicle
of expression *within* the group, communicating and fixing certain
values of religious, social, and moral life through the emotional
suggestiveness of forms" (ibid., 287; emphasis added).

Highly developed at Temple Shalom, style cuts across all facets
of institutional life. Stylistic concern is frequently indicated through
the categorization of a given or potential act or expression as being
either "a Temple Shalom thing to do" or "not a Temple Shalom thing
to do." For example, most members would probably argue that loudness
or uproariousness is "not a Temple Shalom thing to do," while good
art on the walls is most definitely "Temple Shalom." These standards
serve to set boundaries, as they help to furnish self-identity. Hence
a member mockingly suggested that at a neighboring synagogue "the
first thing you see is a cluttered bulletin board and a gift shop display";
by implication, such a statement conveyed the perceived aesthetic
distinctiveness of Temple Shalom. As one of the rabbis commented:

> There is a seriousness about beauty here. There is a feeling that
> there is no reason why art on the walls should not be of good
> quality, why the building should not be maintained well, why a

bulletin or sign should not be nice rather than sloppily put up. There is a concern with the harmony of the setting.

Indeed, the art on display is of excellent quality and the form of display is professional. The members' handbook lists prize artistic possessions and states that "art is an integral part of our temple environment. Paintings, drawings, lithographs, and artifacts are displayed to correspond with current themes, moods, or seasons." Art, then, is one form that reflects Temple Shalom's style. As stipulated earlier, style reflects a group's gestalt and is not limited to one or another sphere of expression or behavior. Food and fashion are other important stylistic expressions at the Temple. Both display "understated elegance," "class," nonostentatiousness.

While the members' handbook, on the one hand, gloats that "Oneg Shabbat at Temple Shalom is legendary. Such a spread!" it elsewhere argues for simplicity during bar/bat mitzva celebrations:

> The temple encourages a simple expression of warmth and joy, executed with modesty and tastefulness. . . . No ceremony, caterer or photographer is necessary to confer this status upon a thirteen-year old.

A stylistic, as well as an ideological, conviction is being expressed here, not unlike the rabbis' call for the "appropriateness of dignity and simplicity during these events." The manner of conduct is thereby prescribed.

Clothing likewise expresses good taste, stylishness, but moderation. Temple Shalom is therefore seen to reflect a particular style: It is seen as unique "in that it is a quiet, understated place. . . physically and emotionally."

Indeed, if style is an expression of collective feeling, as well as ideological commitments, emotional containment is characteristic at Temple Shalom. Opposed to things being "shmaltzy," a member typifies Temple Shalom as "a very classy place. Things are done well here. . . efficient in the way it does things, well mannered, very ordered." The way it does things is paramount, for as style stresses form over content, one of its major elements is its execution, or the technical form it conveys (Kroeber 1957, 30).

Committed to excellence, "quality control," and the conviction that "people are entitled to the best," Temple Shalom's style requires a dedication to civility as a principal ingredient. Dignity, "good taste," modesty, understatement, good manners, and polish are all elements in civility and are all ready characterizations of Temple Shalom. The opposite stylistic orientation—incivility—is often associated in members' minds with other Jewish institutions, consequently setting Temple Shalom apart. Among these marks of incivility are spontaneity, ethnicity, ostentation, sloppiness, shmaltz. In one member's opinion, Temple Shalom's uniqueness inheres in the

> difference in the level of behavior. . . it is higher than in other places. [The congregants] are polite, well-spoken. There is a certain "class," a style here. It's better than what other people have done.

Temple Shalom's preoccupation with civility and high performance reflects, perhaps, a modern aesthetic. As Cuddihy argues, entry into modernity by Jews and other non-Westerners has entailed an adaptation in personal comportment, a preoccupation with "respectability," and a commitment to "niceness": "Intensity, fanaticism, inwardness—too much of *anything*, in fact—is unseemly and bids fair to destroy the fragile solidarity of the surface we call civility" (Cuddihy 1974, 13–14). The "Protestant Etiquette" (Cuddihy 1978, 5) may thus explain Temple Shalom's preoccupation with good taste and refinement, for, according to the cantor, the concern to be always "in good taste" means "to be generally 'non-offensive.' "

Stylistic adherence to this social aesthetic thus communicates to Temple Shalom's members, not only a commitment to Western adaptation, but also a prescription to shun cultural ethnocentrism. Ethnicity, whether in food, dance, or gesture is not part of the cultural fare at Temple Shalom. Particularisms of this kind are found to be embarrassing and possibly crude. Perhaps this is so, as Cuddihy (1974) suggests, because such ethnicity is "too Jewish," that is, it reflects a social aesthetic that is incivil, appropriate in the shtetl but not in middle-class America. Temple Shalom sees itself "beyond Yiddishkeit."

Social class is surely another source of Temple Shalom's style. Beauty, art, excellence, understated elegance are the marks of the financially comfortable. As one of the rabbis suggests:

> There is a bourgeois quality of the upper middle class here. . . a reflection of their life style. The Temple is congruent stylistically with their homes. This is not always so pretty; these are the pace-

setters. When people say that this temple has style and it's different, and we're proud of it, they're really saying: "Well, here we are in the upper middle class in its rare regions."[3]

Congregants feel that Temple Shalom has had a reputation in the larger community of being an exclusive institution, set apart by wealth and insularity. The evaluation of Temple Shalom as "country club" is painful to the current membership, and they work hard to deny its accuracy for the present time. For example, the members' handbook states:

> At Temple Shalom, membership is open to all individuals and families in the Jewish community who agree to support the temple through annual dues. Limited financial circumstances are not an obstacle, however, for comfortable arrangements can always be made. *In short: you don't have to be rich to belong.* (emphasis added)

While it is true, then, that money, as such, is not a determining factor for potential membership, Temple Shalom's style reflects a gestalt that assumes good taste, sophistication, elegance, and non-ethnicity— all characteristics of a particular socioeconomic and educational status. It may be suggested, therefore, that members who, by virtue of upbringing and/or current economic well-being, best match Temple Shalom's style in their private lives feel the greatest attraction to and comfort at Temple Shalom. As one of the rabbi's statements suggested, the Temple's style is a reflection of these members' intentionality.

In sum, in various ways style at Temple Shalom serves to construct communal identity. By evolving a very particular and self-evident style, the synagogue marks itself off from surrounding, alternative institutions that might theoretically claim the loyalty of the membership. As a tool in the construction of "institutional awe," (Kanter 1972, 113) style also expresses and defines, in an active manner, the mentality and identity of members. Style serves to tell congregants who they are by virtue of their Temple Shalom membership.

The various mechanisms that constitute the cult of uniqueness— the Temple Shalom family and its elaboration, the differentiation from the Jewish community in specific ways, and the evolution of a very particular style—nourish the image that "Temple Shalom is the Rolls Royce of synagogues." It has been suggested that through these mechanisms Temple Shalom constructs an identity for itself and its members by setting itself apart from similar institutions and, in so doing, establishing itself as unique, special, and, by implication, better. A few members acknowledge that though their synagogue is indeed special, they do not feel that it is thereby superior, for they feel uncomfortable with this moral posture. There is appeal, however, in the insight from the sociology of deviance that self-identity frequently emerges in contradistinction to alternative identity possibilities (see, for example, J. Douglas 1970; Erikson 1966; Kanter 1972). A moral evaluation is inescapable in this perspective, for the specialness attributed to the self (or to one's institution) is consciously or unconsciously contrasted with the negative evaluations of the other. As J. Douglas asserts:

> Each individual gains in moral worth to the extent that others lose in moral worth, and vice versa . . . one can be considered to be moral or respectable only if there are others, not identified with oneself, who are considered to be immoral or disreputable. . . . To the extent, then, that each individual does want to construct this moral image of himself, he is necessarily committed to a competitive struggle to morally upgrade himself and morally downgrade others (not identified with himself). (1970, 6)

Given the voluntary basis of synagogue membership in America and the "market economy" (Luckmann 1967, 98–99) of Jewish and non-Jewish institutions vying for affiliation, it is no surprise that competition adds to the process of comparison and contrast so well articulated at Temple Shalom in its struggle for self-definition.

Temple Shalom as Community

Membership in a synagogue can have a variety of different meanings for people. The fact that this is a Jewish institution creates a more complex analytic problem in determining personal motivations for belonging. Roughly, we could say that the quest for Jewish community involves a desire to belong to a specific institution—such as Temple Shalom—but more broadly, to form part of a larger gestalt, the Jewish community. The latter is a construct rather than a specific reality today, for it refers in people's minds not only to the organized Jewish institutions in a particular city but, in some sense, to all of

Jewry, past and present, local and international, real and mythical. The Jewish community is, in this way, a somewhat inchoate heir to the religious tradition, historical experience, cultural richness, and political situation of the Jewish people. The synagogue is seen as the central institution of Jewish life in America today; hence, membership in one may be motivated by a variety of cognitive and emotional associations.

Clearly Temple Shalom does not act as a community, as earlier defined, for all its members. Kanter (1972, 68) suggests that individuals orient themselves to a particular community in three basic modes: instrumentally—with respect to the costs and rewards of belonging; affectively—with respect to the emotional attachment to other members; and morally—with respect to the moral compellingness of the norms and beliefs of the system.

Most members are probably instrumentally related to Temple Shalom, in that their association is based largely on their need to send their children to religious schools and/or to have a place to attend during the high holidays. For others, this instrumental link is combined with affective or moral orientations. As we have seen, many members freely cite the excellence of other members or the perceived social activist character of the congregation. Others note the special style as the reason for membership.

Very active members, those most committed to the institution, attach themselves to Temple Shalom through all three modes of orientation. These congregants tend to view Temple Shalom as their principal community. While many hold membership in other institutions, the level of commitment to Temple Shalom, in terms of time and emotional investment, is far greater. As one member declares, "There are three major elements in my life: my family, my business, and my temple. The Temple is certainly the central group in my life."

For some members, belonging to Temple Shalom was a sufficiently high priority that they shaped their lives around it in particular ways. One couple, for example, looked for a home only within a designated radius of the Temple. Membership at Temple Shalom was therefore determinative of their place of residence. In similar fashion, another couple at one point considered moving to another city for occupational advance. Having visited the various synagogues in the prospective new city, they decided not to move because none compared favorably to Temple Shalom.

One member asserts that, by bringing people together, Temple

Shalom meets his needs for community, as such, and not necessarily his Jewish needs. More typically, however, members feel that Temple Shalom furnishes a sense of Jewish identity as it answers their needs for community. The following remarks, offered by three members, indicate such a sentiment:

> It is a place to find roots. This is a pretty rootless kind of city, and at Temple Shalom I find connection, involvement, participation; it means being a part of a community and a tradition.

> Temple Shalom fortifies what it means to be a Jew. With those people at the Temple that I feel close to, I feel I can express the same feelings about things. . .community feelings. It helps me with my identification as a Jew very much.

> The reality of twentieth-century America, being such a pluralistic society, is that people don't live in ghettoes or shtetls. Without a community, I don't see how one can maintain one's Jewish identity. So the synagogue plays that role in part. It helps maintain certain Jewish feelings.

For these and other people, Temple Shalom serves as a port of entry into Judaism, for it furnishes a community situation that seems to meet people's needs for sociability in a setting that is Jewish. Hence, members frequently note that the "spirit of openness" of Temple Shalom gives people the freedom to discover or rediscover their Judaism in their own personal way, without dogmatic pressures. As one congregant puts it, "I feel loyal and indebted to Temple Shalom for offering me a chance and a facility to return to Judaism on my own terms, to find a Jewish identity of my own." In like manner, another congregant feels that "Temple Shalom created an atmosphere in which I as a very nonidentified Jew could explore Judaism."

As with the ideological constituents of Jewishness at Temple Shalom, it is unclear for members what precisely is substantively Jewish about the communal nature of their institution, other than the fact that it is a synagogue. References are sometimes made, as above, to the tradition or to Jewish feelings, but these comments remain at a vague rather than a precise, concrete level. One member, for example, joins aesthetic to ideological elements in addressing this issue when she says, "Temple Shalom has class, style, a kind of quiet dignity that I associate with being Jewish: the courage to say what you believe in, to say what you think." There is a readiness in this statement to identify as Jewish predispositions that have multiple and preexisting sources in people's consciousness.

These issues point to the radical change in the nature of Jewish community that Temple Shalom represents when seen against the backdrop of traditional Jewish society. In Jewish traditional society, the Jewish world view largely constituted personal consciousness, informing thought, as well as standards for action; the group superseded the individual in import and power.

As part of the modern world, however, Temple Shalom's function is seen as providing "whatever the individual is looking for in terms of religious experience." Or, according to another congregant, the synagogue "should provide a format for people to practice their religion *consistent with their own ideologies*" (emphasis added). In fact, while one of the rabbis suggests that the function of the synagogue is "to serve God, to preserve Jewish life, and to serve the needs of Jews," he adds:

> I clearly identify with the latter of these emphases. When confronted with practical decisions between an abstract notion of Judaism and concrete individuals who stand before me, I choose the individuals. . . . At some point I made the decision that I was primarily going to be concerned with the needs of people.

This view reflects a commitment to humanism and individualism over other considerations.

It is clear that in all these responses the individual is seen to be paramount, with the institution having an obligation to serve personal needs, rather than the obverse. While this is an expression of modern sensitivities, it also reveals commitments to Reform's pro-individualistic proclivities.

The tension between individualism and community arises when there is insufficient commonality in the group to integrate the members in a meaningful manner. The disruption of traditional society, the individualism of modernity and of the Reform movement specifically, and the privatistic orientation of contemporary America have led to the weakening of a Jewish communal center. The personal and the private have displaced previously communal and public facets of Jewish life.

An example from Temple Shalom's bulletin illustrates this problem in the form of a letter to the congregation written by the president of the board of trustees:

> How lovely it is to celebrate Shabbat with a Bar or Bat Mitzvah
> and to share the joy of the family on this special occasion. And
> yet, many of us hesitate to attend a Bar/Bat Mitzvah to which we
> have not been invited, in the mistaken notion that our presence
> would be an intrusion on a private event.
>
> A Bar or Bat Mitzvah is not a private event but is always
> observed in the context of a regular service. Through this symbolic
> rite of passage into adulthood, the Bar or Bat Mitzvah accepts the
> heritage and responsibilities of our faith. And the perpetuation of
> Judaism is promised.
>
> Such a ceremony, therefore, should be looked upon as a special
> community event for rejoicing. Each of us honors the occasion,
> the family, and the community by our attendance.

The fact that members of Temple Shalom stay away from services
during such a traditionally communal celebration suggests people's
detachment from a public, communal form of social life in favor of
privatism and personalism. As significant, however, is the disruption
in communal continuity signalled when congregants abstain from
attending a ceremony specifically designed to integrate the bar or bat
mitzva into the adult religious community. The bar or bat mitzva thus
faces a gathering of people—relatives, friends, and neighbors—which
frequently outnumbers Temple Shalom members precisely at the
moment of his or her intended entry into Jewish adulthood and
communal responsibility.

As we have seen, the construction of identity at Temple Shalom
takes place in part through various mechanisms that evolve around
the cult of uniqueness. These mechanisms, including the highly
developed elaboration of style, are primarily functional and formal
in nature, stressing expressive rather than substantive elements. A
concern with content is not absent, however, as one of the rabbis
suggests:

> I'm sometimes troubled by the lack of substance behind the style.
> What we do, we do very well, but I'd like our bar mitzva kids to
> know more....The feelings and attitudes are good, and the
> relationships are solid most of the time. But there isn't enough
> Judaism. There isn't enough time for the rabbis to study, to attend
> to our growth in faith and belief....There should be more time

for adult studying. What is done is done with a good deal of integrity. I see now people who hunger for more; they are ready to have more. We need to help them get more.

Some members express dissatisfaction over the lack of "real content" in the religious school education their children receive. Yet the reigning position, articulated by a member of the religious school committee, seems to be that "at our religious school we are trying to stress kids' experience, to be, to be open." Another congregant suggests that the religious school teaches the "spirit of Judaism" and hence offers a positive attitude for children about Judaism. Yet, at a special service, confirmation-age youth (15–16 years old) suggested that they had not been given enough instruction about the Jewish view of things to be able to function in the world informed by a Jewish value perspective. Dissatisfaction with the level of Jewish content at Temple Shalom is most forcefully illustrated by a question directed at the rabbis by the synagogue's president: "Why is it that people who are serious about Judaism have to go outside the Temple to study?"

The tensions between form and content are raised here to illustrate Cuddihy's (1974, 121–34) contention that modernity is more concerned about *how* things are done rather than about *what* is done. Translating this dilemma into Durkheimian terms, it might be suggested that the source of solidarity at Temple Shalom is principally found in form and style rather than in substantive understanding and lived- out expressions of a Jewish world view. While political liberalism does serve as a source of commonality, we have seen that its specific links to Judaism are somewhat tenuous. Furthermore, a strong behavioral expression of liberalism is missing among congregants. The uniqueness of Temple Shalom, most particularly its style, largely serves as the group's collective conscience, which in ages past was constituted by a religious umbrella that informed consciousness, life style, and identity. This equation is not altogether fitting, for there is a sufficient undercurrent of discontent about the lack of content at Temple Shalom to suggest that the need for substance remains. So, while Temple Shalom largely integrates its members through functional, stylistic, and formalistic mechanisms, the integration is not complete and is subject to troubled reflection and personal unhappiness for some.

The construction of community at Temple Shalom is complicated by a factor that emerges naturally from the Temple's orientation toward individualism, privatism, and formalism. The synagogue hesitates to impose communal demands on individuals, fearful to be seen as coercive in any way. It is difficult, therefore, to ascertain the depth of loyalty or commitment that members give to it. Commitment ultimately means the willingness to sacrifice personal need for the sake of a larger cause. Suggesting that "at Temple Shalom you can be a Jew without being committed," a member made an incisive analysis that seems to cut to the core of this dilemma. Her analysis, closely paraphrased below, merits scrutiny:

> In my opinion, being a committed Jew involves three activities: (1) study, (2) doing moral good in the community, and (3) the observance of ritual so it becomes part of the fabric of your life.
>
> 1. At Temple Shalom study is offered on the surface, without internalizing it. There is no learning of Hebrew. The rabbis give you ideology so you don't have to think yourself. It is like becoming a costume-wearer[4] without going through the difficulties and ambivalence that this elicits in you.
>
> 2. In terms of social action, at Temple Shalom you don't have to do anything yourself. The reputation of the Temple carries you. You don't do anything. Warm bodies are what is needed. At Temple Shalom, there are bells that ring, but there is no real substance in terms of commitment to moral good, except for a few people.
>
> 3. Ritual needs to be internalized. We've lost the ability to have ritual be unself-conscious. We keep outward vestiges...we Westernize it, clean it up. The religious school committee members don't want too much Hebrew because that alienates from Western culture...that's lack of commitment.
>
> At Temple Shalom, lack of commitment means that we don't go through life's highs and lows together. The individual has need of community but has no one to cry with when there is a death, no one to rejoice with when there is a simcha [celebration].

In this critique, the congregant argues that Temple Shalom asks nothing from its members and consequently the latter do not reap, in her view, the promises and possibilities of community. In her opinion, the Temple makes no demands to study, to do moral good, to observe ritual. She suggests that there is talk about substance but that there is no real substance; that there is action but that this is limited and becomes the expression of a vicarious Jewish identity. This member has intuited the nature of modern community as Philip Rieff (1968) sees it.

For Rieff, the premodern age was characterized by "positive communities," those that "offer some sort of salvation to the individual through participant membership." Salvation here refers to an experience that transforms all personal relations by subordinating them to agreed communal purposes. By contrast, the modern period is typified by "negative communities," where individual goals are not part of the collective agenda. Arguing from a psychoanalytic perspective, Rieff (1968, 71–78) suggests that whereas positive communities integrate the individual through guilt, negative communities integrate through information only, as they demand no sacrifice from the individual. Because the self ultimately is the source of authority, the community in modern times fails to integrate the individual in a meaningful or lasting fashion.

It is not necessary, in my view, to embrace Rieff's vision of modernity so literally as to assume that no positive communities are possible. Indeed, contemporary writers like Kelley (1972, 157–58) believe that modern institutions can certainly act as communities that furnish meaning and integration to individuals, provided they place some demands upon them. Kelly suggests that a need of many contemporaries is for more structured lives that give shape and significance to existence. He maintains that the failure of many communities is their unwillingness to ask anything of their members.

The modern world differs from its traditional counterpart, among other ways, in its rich pluralism. In forming personal identity, the individual has many opportunities to join voluntary associations in search of meaning. Many Jews make attachments to Jewish institutions as a means of identification with a collective that transcends them. As we have seen, at Temple Shalom people join and stay for a variety of reasons. The institution serves as a port of entry or reentry into Judaism for some. While an attenuated Jewish profile makes this a possibility for some members, others suffer from a need to find more substance, to encounter greater communal demands, to celebrate the self more actively in a public forum. These members ask for commitment: They wish to find Jewish meanings that will allow them to locate personal concerns in collective goals.

SIX

Conclusions

The Sacralization of Identity

Modernity places all kinds of stresses on personal and collective identity. Rapid social change, physical mobility, pluralism, relativism, and secularism conspire against the stability of people's identity. Traditionally, religion played a central role in fixing personal and group identity, since "stability, continuity and coherence [were] provided by commitment to a set of religious symbols" (Bellah 1965, 173; for related discussions, see also Bellah 1970; Berger 1969; Bruner 1965, 31–57; Durkheim 1964; Eliade 1959). Secularization and competing visions of truth and value have weakened the role of religion in shaping and fixing identity.

But, even in the modern age, it may be argued that religion still has the potential to fix identity, to bring stability to the self or the group in the face of a rapidly changing environment. Through mechanisms of sacralization, religion can symbolically transport the individual or the group into a larger context, providing meaning and significance that transcend the here and now. Ritual, myth and theology, and commitment to a particular set of interpretations and values are some of the ways in which religion sacralizes mundane experience and fixes identity (Mol 1979).

Contemporary Jews experience the pressures of modernity along with their non-Jewish counterparts. The complexity of Jewish culture and the Jewish historical experience—including a late entry into modernity—add yet further elements to the constitution of Jewish identity.

As an American Reform synagogue in the last quarter of the twentieth century, Temple Shalom presents its members with an opportunity to be Jews, defined in complex, multi-layered, and sometimes inconsistent and unsatisfying ways. In doing so, Temple

Shalom joins company with the many institutions of our contemporary landscape that struggle with questions of religious meaning and identity in a secularized culture that offers no a priori, foolproof definitions of what it means to be a Jew. Temple Shalom is thus put in the business of *constructing* identity for its members.

In every area of synagogue life explored in this study, Temple Shalom is involved in the sacralizing of identity. Its ideology, so deeply connected to political liberalism, negotiates a transformation from the simply political to the religious by its ongoing commitment to the Jewish prophetic tradition. Liberal values are seen as deeply Jewish because they are identified with the pronouncements of the Hebrew prophets. The voices of contemporary social reformers are assimilated to the parlance of the biblical visionaries. Identification with the prophetic tradition—central in the Reform movement as a whole—sacralizes identity in yet another way: It effects a tie with the ancient Jewish past, as well as with a particular religious impetus, temporally linking contemporary Jews with a rich ancestry.

Ritual at Temple Shalom sacralizes identity by linking the members' experience to those of Jews across time and space, namely, through its liturgical order and use of Hebrew in prayers and songs; through its celebration of Jewish holidays in the company—imaginatively conceived—of all Jews, past and present; and through symbolism drawn from the tradition, most evident in the Chaverim service, more attenuated in the normative service.

Personal identity is also sacralized in the Temple's communal experience. We have seen that much attention is paid to characteristics that distinguish this synagogue from others, that make it unique and special. Mechanisms of the cult of uniqueness function to commit members to Temple Shalom, to anchor individuals emotionally to this particular community and away from others. And, in fact, individuals continually remark on their attachment to Temple Shalom because of its uniqueness. In these ways, a sacralization of *Temple Shalom* identity is effected. A sacralization of *Jewish* identity is obtained as well, however, in discussions of Temple Shalom as part of the Jewish community. Often a construct rather than a concrete referent is meant by the "Jewish community," yet functionally such references serve to move individual members from personal, individual concerns and associations to a sense of transpersonal belonging and import.

The existence of these mechanisms of sacralization notwithstanding, we have seen that issues related to Jewish content have been problematic at Temple Shalom, often leading to a precarious sense of Jewish identity for its members. While the synagogue acts as a port of entry into Judaism for some people, its definitions of Jewishness appear sparse or insufficient to others. One way we might proceed in evaluating Temple Shalom's effectiveness in shaping and fixing the identity of its members is to examine its evaluative assumptions.

The cluster of values that shapes the identity of a community— partially or completely—may be called the community's ethic. We have noted that this ethic is expressed in the manner that its members characterize ways of saying "we" (see the Introduction, p. 4). The ethic has three temporal dimensions: its roots are in the past, a tradition that furnishes its values, but it also contains prescriptions for present action and a vision of the future (Sellers 1975, 40).[1] An ethic is not permanent, hence the community's identity is bound to be changeable. An ethic is no longer fitting when a community's members fail to be integrated by it, or, to put it another way, when there is a wide chasm between subjective experience and objective definitions.

In looking at Temple Shalom across ideological, ritualistic, and communal expressions, we shall examine some central evaluative assumptions and assess the goodness of fit between them, the members' experience, and the temper of the times, since the experience of modern American Jews is closely related to modern, as well as American, circumstances.[2]

The Liberal Ethic

Insofar as Temple Shalom promotes many of the commitments of early Reform Judaism, its assumptions reflect a liberal ethic. That is, many of its values are drawn principally from nineteenth-century liberalism: faith in progress, universalism, the brotherhood of man, individualism, rationalism, humanism. The prophetic tradition in Judaism is tied to these liberal values in linking the latter to Jewish concerns. This, in effect, assumes a commitment to social justice and social activism.

Universalism and Individualism

Universalism was part of the Enlightenment's contribution to

European and American modernizing culture at the time of the rise and development of Reform. The embrace of universalism was therefore the intellectual assent to a different basis for culture, namely, the use of reason as opposed to tradition as the norm for cultural authority. Concomitantly, individualism was accepted as the alternative to the corporate, traditional structure in discerning truth and in structuring personal identity. Guided by the laws of reason, the individual intellect was seen to have claims prior to collective wisdom; the intellect's perception of truth, following Kant, required a universalizing principle to legitimize its standing. This provided the intellectual impetus to universalism over particularism, the commitment to a universal brotherhood of man versus the parochial limitations of particularist loyalties.

Reform's liberal convictions also arose out of the sociological need of many Jews to integrate into the modern liberal culture of Western Europe. The rejection of particularistic and ethnic Jewish traits was an essential requirement of this transition, for entry into Western society was predicated upon ethnic and national neutrality: The host country was to command sole national allegiance (see the "Transactions of the Parisian Sanhedrin," 1956). The atomization of the Jew began thus, as religion came to be the single object of distinctiveness among Western European Jews; otherwise, they were to become acculturated citizens of Western European nations.

Arrival in America perpetuated this pattern. The "melting pot" ideology produced a leveling effect on ethnic particularities as immigrants were urged to become "full-fledged Americans." In fact, the message given to new arrivals was that conformity to the American Way of Life—indeed, conformity to a "White Anglo-Saxon Protestant" ethic—was of the essence. Acceptance into the host country, this time free America, was contingent upon submersion of ethnic distinctiveness (see Novak 1972).

Ideological and sociological currents have, of course, changed since the development of these patterns. In fact, some changes of critical importance have taken place only within the last two decades or so, changes that have challenged the assumptions embraced by early Reform. For one, the rationalist assumption that social contract, in effect, makes communal existence strictly voluntary has been rendered an inappropriate theory in light of current knowledge (Nisbet 1953, 224–32). It is now recognized that individuals are inherently social and that the symbols and meanings that inform their thinking and imaging come from the various communities to which they belong. While individuals have a capacity to transcend the loyalties of specific communities, they also are unable to live for long outside of social contexts. Personal identity is forged and maintained through commitment to social institutions and collective ideas (Mol 1976, 216–32). Hence, far from being voluntarily sociable, human beings are inextricably tied to particularistic collectivities.

The cultural pluralism of the last two decades in America has also challenged the universalistic assumptions of a uniform American character. The celebration of cultural distinctiveness, initiated most directly by the black community in the sixties, broke the illusion of a "melting pot" that presumably reflected universally held American values and symbols. Indeed, the seventies were called the "decade of the ethnics" (Novak 1972, 3). That is a characterization of cultural particularity of groups whose distinctive cultural orientations and psychological sensibilities until then remained in good measure submerged from the public arena. Undoubtedly, the loss of confidence in the American way of life, instigated by Vietnam and Watergate, was an important contributing factor to the celebration of particularity.

Novak (1974) suggests that the older, "universalist" model in America produced the "liberal personality." The latter assumes the individual's access to universal reason and the consequent disvaluing of finite communities, for these are seen as parochial and limiting of individual freedom. This personality tends to be

> atomic, rootless, mobile, and to imagine itself as "enlightened" in some superior and especially valid way. Its exaggerated individualism leads instantly to an exaggerated sense of universal community. (Novak 1974, 44)

By contrast, Novak suggests that the "pluralistic personality" counters individualism with "self-conscious and disciplined participation in specific cultural traditions, institutions, loyalties, and symbol systems" (ibid., 44). He goes on to say that

> a human being cannot properly pretend to be infinite or universal; he or she necessarily participates in concrete cultural traditions, institutions, loyalties, and symbols systems. . . .Where the liberal personality seeks a virtually direct ascent from individual will to universality, commonality and rationality, the pluralistic personality

finds a certain peace in particularity, and seeks in particularity itself
a method of "analogous depth"—a method of going deeply into
one's own tradition in order to find a way to "pass over," by a system
of analogies, into the comparable voyages taken by others into their
own traditions. (ibid., 44)

Schooled in the convictions of early Reform, Temple Shalom's
ethic reflects a system of assumptions and values that favors the construction of a liberal over a pluralistic personality in its members. It
is not that Temple Shalom denies the fact of Jewish peoplehood, for
example. But the manner of presenting Jewish particularity attenuates
such particularity. Judaism is defined as prophetic Judaism, hence a
Judaism with universalistic ends. Particularistic symbolism—visual,
liturgical, ritual—is minimal, giving rise to a very special type of
Jewishness. Jewish peoplehood is rendered more as an historical
memory than as an active identification with other Jews today or as
an engagement with particularistic meanings.

Temple Shalom's maintenance of the liberal ethic and, by extension, of the liberal personality, reflects assumptions that are important
to understand. Despite the move in the larger society to acknowledge
the limitations of a strictly universalistic, individualistic ethic and the
changes in American culture which invite cultural particularism, we
have seen that Temple Shalom has held fast to its early commitments.
It has not actively joined the Reform movement's turn to the appreciation of particularity and recovery of the tradition.

In part, such a decision, made by the rabbis, represents a religious
conviction. While it is true that human beings are inevitably members
of collectivities less inclusive than a universal community, the potential
danger in the celebration of such particularity is the danger of idolatry.
That is, when particularistic values take precedence over ultimate
values, the "we group" sets itself up as ultimate. The rabbis are aware
that proximate ethnic commitments often lose sight of ultimate values.
Hence, they refuse to allow what they see as the religio-ethical
mandates of Judaism to be used in the service of particularistic
interests. This concern is not a purely theoretical one, for the last
decade has seen a shift in the Jewish community toward a politically
more conservative, inner-directed, self-interested posture, as in the
case of affirmative action, for example.

Yet the rabbis' attack on Jewish particularism and their continued
commitment to universalism has not necessarily led members to

involvement in issues of universal concern or social activism. A greater valuing of particularism—whether through greater knowledge of the tradition or more ritual observance or greater ethnic celebration— need not be the major contributor to the narcissistic closing-off to the problems, values, and concerns of humanity at large. In fact, if Novak (1974, 43) is correct, depth gained in one's own community— through participation in its traditions, institutions, loyalties, and symbolic systems—encourages one to "pass over" into the symbolic worlds of others, for purposes of understanding, communication, and cooperation. In a similar vein, Bellah et al. (1985, 152–55) urge people to dip into their "communities of memory" in order to discover a moral language—unavailable outside of an historical tradition— that will connect the self to the group and the group to the larger social order.

The major point here is that Temple Shalom's current ethic, with its emphasis on universalism and the liberal personality, renders a weakened Jewish identity. While we have noted that Temple Shalom sacralizes Jewish identity by identifying it with political liberalism, the content of that identity is precariously grounded. For, while many adult members were raised in homes suffused with the spirit of liberalism, they are not nearly as well versed in the contents of Judaism. We may recall that most members, rather uneducated in Jewish matters, experience a feeling of ideological incompetence: People cannot defend intellectually their sense of Jewishness and rely completely on the expertise of the clergy.

A sense of continuity, an important element in a stable identity, is also compromised by the lack of greater knowledge of the inherited tradition as future generations have less raw material with which to forge a meaningful Jewish identity. Since the appeal of political ideologies shift with time, greater knowledge of Judaism may need to be prior to any one political ideology if it is to have continuing impact, on this and future generations, as a religious social ethic. Through the understanding of the Jewish tradition, a substantive identity has the chance of emerging to meet political and cultural challenges. This would place individuals in a better position to link what they know about their religious, cultural heritage (whether they agree with it or not) and contemporary values and dilemmas.

In addition, it is not sufficient for the liberal ethic—or any other ethic—to be linked from the pulpit by the clergy as a way to reinforce a particular vision of Judaism. The reliance on experts leads moderns to experience passivity rather than engagement; without existential engagement a solid identity is impossible, especially in light of rapid social and ideological change. A firm link among the past, present, and future can be achieved in consciousness only through existential wrestling with the Jewish tradition itself.

The following statement, which supports this view, appears in the recent "Centenary Perspective" of the Reform movement:

> Reform Jews are called upon to confront the claims of Jewish tradition, however differently perceived, and to exercise their individual autonomy, choosing and creating on the basis of commitment and knowledge. ("Reform Judaism" 1977, 9)

In effect, such a statement calls for the active engagement of congregants in the learning of the tradition, without giving up personal freedom. But, implicit in this statement is the recognition that individual autonomy can be exercised only from a position of knowledge.

Applying this message to Temple Shalom, I would argue that a strong Jewish identity cannot emerge when the intellectual heritage is apprehended through formalistic typification alone. A bona fide confrontation with the past is essential in the constitution of a community's ethic. The tradition need not—and should not—be embraced carte blanche, but it must be understood as a stepping stone in the development of an ethic that must also shape present mandates and future visions.

Rationality

The call for an existentially grounded Jewish identity challenges, as well, another assumption of the liberal ethic, namely, its adulation of rationality. For while reason is a key human given, it alone fails to account for the entirety of human experience, potentiality, or need. Emotion and spirit are equally important in the constitution of identity. This is not to say that such aspects of human personality were unknown prior to the Enlightenment! Rather, they had to be recaptured and relegitimated following the singularly rationalistic stress of that period. Unsurprisingly, movements like romanticism and existentialism, rising in reaction to the Enlightenment's arid rationalism, also failed to give an accurate and balanced account of human nature, erring on the side of emotion and will. In order to furnish lasting identity, therefore, an ethic must engage all levels of human experience.

In its reverence for rationality, Reform Judaism failed to take account, much less appreciate, the "mystical, romantic and historical elements of the religious experience" (Agus 1954, 70). Enamored of reason, and hence of the latter's expression through language, Reform neglected to take due note of the nondiscursive needs of the human psyche: needs for emotive, symbolic, and ritual stimulation and expression.

There are signs at Temple Shalom which indicate that worship services, for example, often fail to engage some of the congregants' multiple needs: These people desire more emotionality, less cognitive content, greater participation, less passivity. The Chaverim service can be seen, in addition to a path to community for its members, as a weathervane of unmet nondiscursive needs. The needs felt by participants in the Chaverim service may be widespread in the congregation as a whole.

Klapp (1969, 3–46) suggests that identity problems in modern society can be explained by the absence of symbolic reference points which enable people to remember and to validate who they are. By contrast, in premodern times personal identity was continually reinforced by reference to stable social groups, collective traditions, religious ritual and other ceremonies, unchanging places, stories and myths, and so forth. The break with meaningful past traditions and the rapid mobility (personal and spatial) of modern society has produced identities that are symbolically impoverished. Present preoccupation with information and technique has often resulted in the neglect of wisdom, expressivity, and the profound human need for meaning.

The Reform movement has moved in recent years toward the reappropriation of past ritual and the celebration of particularistic symbolism. However misused this return may have been in some cases, nonetheless the motivation has been a sound one. Reform has recognized the limitations of its early views that enthroned rationality while rejecting equally significant needs for symbolic anchoring in ritual and symbol (see, for example, Mirsky 1978, 21). Rather than gestures of "mindless traditionalism," as some traditional reappropriations are called at Temple Shalom, these developments may be seen as efforts to regain a dimension of identity and experience unavailable through reason or the word alone. As Mol, for example, suggests, rites are fundamentally different from rational action because "they stabilize through emotional anchorage," while rational action "avoids emotional commitment" (1976, 244).

These insights are reflected in the words of Rabbi Alexander Schindler, president of the Union of American Hebrew Congregations, during his 1983 State of the Union Message to the biennial meeting of that national organization of Reform synagogues:

> The need to cultivate a sense of the sacred within ourselves and in our midst is an aspect of our religious enterprise that has been far too long neglected. . . . I ask merely that we address this issue, urgently, earnestly, and with all the resources of mind and spirit at our command. I ask also that we begin the task by probing within ourselves, by making demands on ourselves. . . . and our fellow congregants too. Then and then only will we have the kind of faith that sustains us, that lifts us above the mundane and the dry-as-dust to that empyrean where the divine abides. (Schindler 1984, 26)

Inasmuch as Temple Shalom's current ethic still champions rationality and attenuates emotive and spiritual dimensions, it fails to integrate members who feel a need for a more balanced orientation. Subjective need fails to find fulfillment in an ultrarational objective reality. A reevaluation of the supremacy of rationality therefore seems to be in order.

Secularism

A movement committed to modernity, Reform embraced modernity's vision of a demystified world, one characterized by rationality and technological progress rather than by transcendence and mystery. In retaining these early Reform assumptions, Temple Shalom remains a modernizing institution, one that partakes of modernity's desacralizing orientation—that is, of secularism. The interpretation of Judaism in singularly ethical terms—that is, through prophetic Judaism—also can be seen as the modernizing of tradition. The traditional consciousness involved belief in a supernatural reality and a set of actions that conformed to that belief. The secularization of that consciousness, with the advent of modernity, meant that, in order to retain a Judaism that fit within the secular nature of the modern world, its terms had to be secular. Justice, the doing of good deeds, being kind and caring to others, can all be done outside of a supernaturally ordered world (see Berger 1979, 114–15). Prophetic Judaism *as an idea* arose only during the nineteenth century, in response to contemporary, modernizing intellectual currents and out of a wish to provide a new basis for Reform Judaism that was as old and authoritative as the Torah (Jacob 1979, 43). In so doing, Reform, in practice, purged Judaism of legalistic, pietistic, and spiritual expressions, despite the fact that prophetic Judaism, as such, was defined by various thinkers in a variety of ways (ibid.).

Yet the heart of religion, in the end, rests with religious experience, the encounter between the human and the transcendent. The prophets themselves, in a most dramatic way, represent those charismatic figures who spoke their words of judgment inspired by supernatural mandates. In an ironic adaptation to modernity, the prophetic message is secularized when it is delivered strictly as an historical legacy, cut off from its religious grounding.

It is true that the modern world by and large favors an indifference to spirituality and supernatural concerns. Yet the needs of human beings for transcendence and meaning remain intact, not necessarily for transcendence in the traditional sense of communion with God, but the need, capacity, and desire to transcend current circumstances, to sacralize life, to seek ultimate concerns. These are signals of transcendence, indications that human beings do not and cannot live within a strictly factual and humanly created world, even in modernity (see Berger 1970; Karff 1979, 94–122).

Individuals at Temple Shalom may not speak of the transcendent, as such, and the rabbis may not address the question of God. Yet affiliation with a synagogue may express for some the wish to be in touch with a reality—a "value center," to use H. R. Niebuhr's (1960, 110) term—that goes beyond the techniques of modern life and offers people values worth living by and a vision of future fulfillment. The existing language of transcendence may no longer ring true at Temple Shalom, yet there is an unmistakably religious search going on by those who inchoately talk about a desire for greater spirituality.

The universe for spiritual exploration is too small at Temple Shalom. Encased in what one rabbi calls "the rigidity of our agnosticism," little room is made to actively explore, verbally or experientially, a spiritual dimension. Dominated by an overly rationalistic zeal, the spiritual level is left dormant. In a culture that does so little to lift the spirit beyond facts, the synagogue has the unique opportunity to address the potentials for meaning, spiritual vitality, and emotional wholeness, in other words, to open up avenues for the expression and experience of a full humanity and a rich Jewish identity.

The Construction of a New Ethic

Temple Shalom's existing ethic is basically an ethic of modernization, one whose assumptions and values principally support a modernizing commitment. Yet today, this ethic fails to integrate its members adequately, judging by its inability to provide a strong Jewish identity that feels comfortable and unselfconscious to many of its members. In addition, as we have seen in preceding chapters, members express dissatisfactions with some aspects of congregational life that represent modern orientations. Perhaps these dissatisfactions fit the larger cultural realization that it is now time to move into a postmodern age, a time to challenge the heretofore unquestioned goodness of modernity's contribution to life, a time to counter the sterility and valuelessness of modern life. This is not necessarily a call for the return to the traditional past as such, that is, to the reactionary's vision of the good life. Rather, it is a call to reevaluate the merits of modern values and to aim beyond them if they have run their course.

It could perhaps be argued that an ethic—as those fundamental values that shape the identity of a group—cannot be constructed at will; that is, like symbols, an ethic cannot be "invented," but it emerges when the situation calls for it, and it dies when it is no longer appropriate (see Tillich 1958, 43, on symbols). But I would suggest that, when an existing ethic insufficiently informs the identity of a community, the community needs to be involved in an active effort of exploration and construction.

In premodern times, identity was typically a given, taken-for-granted matter that gave Jews a world view, images of self, and recipes for conduct. Having entered modernity and adapted rather successfully to it, identity for the Jews, as for their contemporaries, is a process rather than a completed fact. The modern individual, who belongs to a plurality of groups but is defined by none of them completely, is engaged throughout life in a process of self-construction. Berger et al. (1974, 74–79) suggest that personal identity is constructed with the aid of a "life plan," a projection of self into the future. Because the individual lives in a pluralistic environment without a coherent meaning system, identity is not firmly or unshakably grounded; it is therefore open to challenge from alternative life-worlds and hence subject to change. Consequently, the self is subject to ongoing identity crises, certainly a familiar mark of modernity.

The notion of a life plan perhaps can be borrowed as a tool of identity construction in modern collectivities, particularly in potential moral communities like Temple Shalom. The life plan would involve, at the most general level, the evaluation of the community's fundamental assumptions and values, the testing of ways of saying "we." A community's members would collectively ask: What is our past? In what way are we shaped by it? In what way should we be shaped by it? In what way should we be free of it? Who are we now? Do we want that identity? What alternative ways of saying "we" should we consider for our future? For our children's future? What do we believe? What do we abhor? What is significant ritual behavior for us? What is merely rote? What is insufficient? How can we envision alternative ways of being a worshipping community? What is our relationship to other Jewish communities? Is this a satisfying/optimal relationship? How would we like it to be different? What are our values? Our obligations? Do these mesh? What is the relationship between our Jewishness and our attitudes in general? Is the relationship rhetorical or actual? Do we want to change it? How?

Asking questions collectively in designing a communal life plan is the first step in articulating a commitment toward relating past, present, and future. The self-consciousness of the process is one of the costs of modernity for Jews and others. It clearly involves shifting meanings and a measure of insecurity in one's sense of identity. The process also points to a benefit of modernity because it offers freedom and creativity, allowing the individual to exercise personal autonomy and collective cooperation in the realization of personal and communal goals.

Modern individuals, Jewish or not, in most cases will not give up their personal freedom for the sake of full social or cultural integration. They will not willingly relinquish their rationality or their right to question and to challenge in order to combat personal alienation. It is impossible and even undesirable (if one is committed to democratic values) to suggest that moral communities have the possibility of fully embracing the individual into their fold, of submerging personal interests completely for the benefit of the whole. Yet, intermediate solutions are worth exploring.

Durkheim (1966, 361–92), for one, ponders the dilemmas of modernity and of the modern person at length. Aware that individuals need to have a sense of belonging and moral directives to inform their lives, Durkheim concludes that society at large is no longer able to respond to these needs. The size and complexity of modern society, plus the vast distance that exists between the individual and national organs of social control, preclude the moral integration of the individual at that level. Durkheim hence calls for the development of "corporations" or occupational groups to serve as the moral anchors of modern persons. Closer to our own time, a number of voices can be heard calling for the establishment of voluntary associations (Nisbet 1975), intermediate structures (Bellah and Sullivan 1981), or mediating structures (Kerrine and Neuhaus 1979) to allay the sense of alienation and moral dislocation of contemporary people and to engage them in the fabric of public life.

The synagogue, it seems to me, is well equipped to serve the role of the corporation or the intermediate structure. It is an institution that has the potential for providing meaning and value for individuals, purposes of a different order than functional ends alone. The synagogue presents the members with symbols and meanings that transcend institutional boundaries by going back to traditional sources of Judaism and Jewishness and forward toward the promise of group continuity and religious significance. In these ways, it can effectively sacralize identity, lifting it from confusion to clarity, from precarious, ongoing change to stability and substance. Since members are not legislated by the synagogue in the way that they were in traditional times, the individual's commitment and participation in the construction of moral community and the group's ethic is essential.

In the modern world, a world that contains multiple life-worlds and is subject to moral and ideological relativism, individuals are faced finally with an existential challenge. They no longer have automatic location in a particular community but rather have the opportunity to select their communities. This freedom to choose their identity frees them from the coercion and constraints that defined their traditional counterparts. Through selection of and commitment to a community, individuals can hope to escape the alienation that comes with pluralism and the moral uncertainty dictated by relativism.

In a world that presents us with "warring gods" (Weber 1972a, 153), the task may be to find one god, one set of values people can believe in and live by. Such search cannot be a solely individualistic one, however. The construction of a meaningful moral anchor is the task of community; a universe of meaning can never be sustained in the individual's mind alone but in relationship with others who share one's longings and values.

The synagogue can serve as a forum for countering the anomie of modern life, for addressing the war of the gods, and for choosing one god. If the synagogue is to serve this role, it must assist its members in transcending the moral relativity of our times: It must root the individual in an historical and metaphysical reality that gives shape to life's possibilities as it combats the despair engendered by a modern relativism that sees every belief as equally valid and every value as equally good. The search for meaning and order today is thus not a return to the simpler formulations of the past. Rather, it involves the willingness of people to work in their chosen communities to define their possibilities and their boundaries and to commit themselves to them.

As Buber (1950, 135) points out, a community's most fundamental characteristic is a center, a center of meaning and action that links people in the process of collective integration. Commitment to such a center can arise through the response to demands placed on its members, demands to be fully engaged in the task at hand. In the asking of questions, in the struggle to respond to them, in the exchange of views and feelings perhaps an active and engaged sense of communal belonging and Jewish identity can be born at Temple Shalom—and in other such communities—that will forge a substantive sense of group and self.

Notes

Introduction

1. H. Richard Niebuhr died before he could formulate a systematic statement of his ethics. *The Responsible Self* (1963), published posthumously, consists of lectures which explore his methodological and substantive ethical concerns. That book's introduction (pp. 6–41), written by James M. Gustafson, is particularly helpful in clarifying Niebuhr's ethical assumptions and directions.

2. My interest in this study is with questions of Jewish identity more so than with issues of Jewish identification. Jewish identity pertains to a person or a group's sense of self with regard to being Jewish, while identification studies, according to H.S. Himmelfarb, "ask questions about ritual observance, Jewish organizational involvement, attitudes toward Israel, intermarriage, and other matters related to Jewish life" (1982, 57). For other definitional distinctions between these conceptual categories, see Herman (1970, 1977).

3. I recorded notes during the course of most events, except during religious services and a few situations (such as a dinner party) when this would have been inappropriate. Field notes, both written and mnemonic, were comprehensively typed within a day or two following the event. During the first five months, I organized the data in a largely chronological manner, without much attempt to consciously draw out themes or interpretative schemata. However, I inserted theoretical notes amidst the undoctored field notes to raise issues that seemed insightful and that would possibly merit attention later on.

4. Interview data were treated in the same way as observational data; hence, they were transcribed soon after recording. Due to time considerations, paraphrasing rather than literal transcription was done. When necessary, however, I carefully listened to tape recordings for exact quotations. Written documents, sermons, and the observation of physical and spatial aspects of Temple Shalom also served as sources of data.

Formal analysis did not start immediately, due to the exhaustive involvement in data gathering and recording during the first five months. Therefore, it did not significantly overlap with field work during that time period. Half way through the year of investigation, I began to establish files. Following Lofland's (1971, 118–24) model, I typed field notes in triplicate from the beginning. One set of notes remained, in gross fashion, in a chronological file. A second set was organized as a mundane file intended for categorization of broad subjects, interviewees, or activities (e.g., "social action committee meetings," "Rabbi _____," "Purim celebration"). The third set constituted the analytic file, which consisted of data coded along particular analytic categories (e.g., "uniqueness of Temple Shalom," "Judaism and ethical issues"). Field notes were cut up with scissors according to these coded categories and grouped in appropriate files; cross referencing was used when data applied to more than one analytic category.

A frequent review of the various files eventually gave rise to themes that cut across categories and interviewees' responses. Further collection of data and discussion of my findings with members in casual circumstances were used to validate the fit of my conclusions with the experience of the members. This testing of the researcher's interpretations follows Schutz's "postulate of adequacy" (1971, 44).

5. Samuel C. Heilman has written two important ethnographic works on Jewish identity: *Synagogue Life* (1973), and *The People of the Book* (1983). These studies focus on Orthodox identity; the former is based in America, the latter largely in Israel. Heilman works out of the tradition of symbolic interactionism, while my concerns are more pointedly oriented to ideology and consciousness in the construction of Reform identity. There has been a great deal of interest recently in Orthodox and Chassidic Jews and their communities. This book's focus on Reform Jews and their identity is unique at the present time.

Chapter One. The Transformation of Jewish Identity

1. Of necessity this exploration is of a synthetic and thus generalized nature. The interested reader is directed to the references provided in text citations and in the Notes.

2. Useful works on the nature of traditional Jewish society prior to Emancipation include Howe and Greenberg (1973), Katz (1961, 1962), Roskies and Roskies (1975), Rotenstreich (1972), Schulman (1974), Zborowski and Herzog (1962).

3. Useful works on the Jewish move to modernity include Blau (1966), Dawidowicz (1967), Goldscheider and Zuckerman (1984), M. Himmelfarb

(1973), Katz (1961, 1962), Meyer (1967).

4. Internal factors were also significant in the disruption of traditional Jewish society. Especially important was the impact of Chassidism, a treatment of which lies beyond the scope of this discussion (see Dawidowicz 1967; Katz 1961). In the following discussion of the Jewish move to modernity, the stress is placed on the nature of consciousness and personal identity. An interest in mentality therefore supersedes a consideration of infrastructure; ways of "perceiving, expressing, and valuing" (Inkeles and Smith 1974, 16) receive more attention than organizational or institutional configurations.

5. For discussions of these dimensions of modernization, see Berger et al. (1974), Durkheim (1964), Eliade (1959), Luckmann (1967).

6. Useful works on the American Jewish experience include Blau (1976), Borowitz (1973), Davis (1971), Feingold (1974), Glazer (1972), Howe (1976), Jick (1976), Liebman (1973), Neusner (1975, 1978), Sklare (1958, 1972, 1974a, 1974b, 1982, 1983), Sklare and Greenblum (1967), Weisberg (1964).

7. Ashkenazim (a derivative of Ashkenaz, Hebrew for Germany) refers basically to Eastern and Central European Jews whose ancestors presumably first settled in the Rhineland. Its contrasting term is Sephardim (from Sephard, Hebrew for Spain), which denotes descendants of Jews who had settled in the Iberian Peninsula.

8. This is not to deny the recent development of the so-called Jewish religious revival, including a significant increase in religious observance within Orthodoxy and the rise of the *baal teshuva* phenomenon (typically referring to non-Orthodox Jews who have "repented" or "returned" to a strictly observant life style). At the present time, however, these patterns are representative of a small percentage of American Jews. While there seem to be signs of a more general religious revitalization in American Judaism today—including Jewish feminism, return to roots and ritual, chavurot— this ferment does not constitute a return to the precepts, practices, and assumptions of traditional Judaism as such.

Chapter Two. Temple Shalom: Setting and Reform Context

1. Oneg Shabbat refers to the celebration of the Sabbath that follows services. Food and socializing are its principal features.

2. The executive director has retired since the conclusion of the study.

3. It should be noted that Reform was not alone or necessarily unique

in its response to modernizing forces. Other modernizing Jewish movements responded in varying degrees to similar concerns (see, for example, Blau 1966).

Chapter Three. Ideology and Identity

1. This definition follows Samuel Beer's (cited in Bluhm 1974, 6) typification of "political culture." "Ideology" has more generally been used to indicate purposeful or unwitting distortion of the truth in an effort to conceal personal or class interests. For a discussion of definitional controversies, see Bluhm (1974), Feuer (1975), and Mannheim (1936).

2. In this section, the Jewish tradition refers to the specific religio-legal culture of premodern Jewry described in Chapter One. "Traditional" is used as the adjectival referent for that concept.

3. Yarmulke is the Yiddish term for skullcap. The more current term in Jewish circles today is the Hebrew word *kippa*. I chose yarmulke in this context because that was the term used at Temple Shalom. The use of that term is an interesting one, insofar as it carries associations with the tradition of the European past and not with the living tradition to be found either in the State of Israel or among many religiously involved American Jews.

4. Though Temple Shalom expends a great deal of energy on sermons and discussions about the State of Israel and the Middle East, the synagogue's Zionism is tempered by its liberalism. This is expressed through genuine efforts to understand the complexity of the Middle East situation, including the role of the Palestinian people. Such a position does not lead to an unquestioned commitment to Israeli policies, nor to what one member called a "hotly Zionistic" posture.

Chapter Four. Ritual and Identity

1. Ritual, that is, patterned behavior, is not confined to the religious sphere. Anthropologists, sociologists, and psychologists (beginning with Freud's fascination with compulsive behavior) have only recently begun exploring the nature of so-called secular ritual (see for example, Moore and Myerhoff 1977 and Goffman 1967). In this context, however, ritual is used in reference to religiously related phenomena.

2. *Gates of Prayer* (1975), the new Reform prayerbook, is available both in the English (left to right) and Hebrew (right to left) opening styles. While some synagogues have chosen the latter, Temple Shalom's copies are in the English style.

3. On the other hand, the traditional synagogue reserved the seats by the eastern wall to honor the community's rich and powerful members. Moreover, democracy in the traditional synagogue was a male prerogative, as women were required to sit behind a partition (*mechitza*) and played no leadership role in the service. Hence, in this discussion, observations about traditional worship generally reflect the experience of male congregants only.

4. The circumambulation with the Torah takes place at the beginning of the Torah service. Once the rabbi takes a Torah scroll out of the ark and particular blessings are recited, he takes it around to the congregation. It is customary for the worshipper to transmit a kiss to the scroll by using a hand, prayerbook, or prayer shawl as a conduit.

5. The association of the circumambulation with the Torah and idolatry is a familiar one in classical Reform.

6. Clearly, the way that Ducey (1977) uses "interaction ritual" has far greater specificity than Goffman's (1967) use of the term.

Chapter Five. Community and Identity

1. The rabbis represent the essence of modern Judaism for the congregants. To the extent that the latter feel ambivalent about their Jewishness, then, the rabbis personify such a conflict and hence receive mixed evaluations. Heilman makes a similar point in his study of an Orthodox synagogue: "As an embodiment of religious life, the rabbi frequently becomes the focus for the modern Orthodox Jew's ambivalence about his religion" (Heilman 1973, 107).

2. It is not uncommon for Jews to attribute uniqueness to their synagogue and their rabbi, and in this regard Temple Shalom may be expressive of more general American Jewish attitudes. What I see as unique at Temple Shalom, however, is a pervasive *preoccupation* with the perceived uniqueness of every facet of congregational life: the rabbis, the members, the ideology, the art, the style, and so forth. Furthermore, there is widespread agreement among the members about the uniqueness and specialness of these facets of Temple Shalom life. By contrast, it is not uncommon in other synagogues to find political struggles between rabbinic supporters and rabbinic detractors. The exploration of structural support for the cult of uniqueness which follows (in the discussions of differentiation from the Jewish community and of style) reveals the actual, as well as the perceived, ways in which Temple Shalom has established itself as unique or different in the context of the broader Jewish community around it.

3. A concern with style and uniqueness appears to be common in other upper middle-class religious institutions. Similar observations were offered to me by a rabbi who has served an east coast synagogue and by a member of a west coast Episcopal church.

4. This member was probably making reference to the use of ritual vestments, in general, and to the issues raised in the Temple's controversy around the use of skullcaps (see Chapter Three).

Chapter Six. Conclusions

1. Sellers's (1975, 66) concept of community is far more inclusive than mine, for he uses it to encompass the common life of American society as a whole. Nonetheless, I feel that his model for discerning the basis of communal identity is applicable to smaller social units, as well.

2. My move at this point from description to prescription likely falls prey to the naturalistic fallacy, since, logically, prescription cannot be derived from description. I take issue with the applicability of this law of philosophical ethics within the realm of "the world of daily life," to use Schutz's (1971, 208) term. It seems to me that prescriptions are indeed shaped by people's experiences and by the stories that inform their lives.

Glossary

Every Hebrew or Yiddish word has been translated or defined at its first appearance in the text. For easy reference, the following list includes terms that appear more than once.

bar/bat mitzva (Hebrew): son/daughter of the commandment; a boy or girl reaches this stage, usually at the age of thirteen, when a ceremony formalizes passage into adult Jewish responsibility

bima (Hebrew): raised platform in front of the sanctuary; location for the lectern, ark, and its Torah scrolls

chavura (Hebrew): fellowship group

cheder (Yiddish): school

Diaspora (Greek): the dispersion or scattering of the Jewish people from the land of Israel following the Exile

Halacha (Hebrew): "the way"; the corpus of Jewish law

Haskala (Hebrew): the Jewish Enlightenment

kehilla (Hebrew): "community"; organ of communal self-government in pre-Emancipation Jewish social life

maskil (Hebrew): "enlightened one"; refers to the Jew who embraced the Jewish Enlightenment

menora (Hebrew): ritual candelabrum

mitzva (Hebrew): commandment

Oneg Shabbat (Hebrew): celebration of the Sabbath following services

Shabbat (Hebrew): the Sabbath

Shema (Hebrew): central prayer, asserting the unity of God

shtetls (Yiddish): small towns in Eastern Europe where Jews frequently
   constituted a significant part of the population

shuckling (Yiddish): swaying in prayer

Talmud (Hebrew): the codified oral law, along with rabbinic commentary
   and analysis

yarmulke (Yiddish): skullcap; worn by traditional Jewish males at all times
   as a sign of reverence

yeshiva (Hebrew): an academy of advanced Jewish learning

Bibliography

Agus, J. B. *Guideposts in modern Judaism: An analysis of current trends in Jewish thought.* New York: Bloch Publishing Co., 1954.

Babcock, B. A. Introduction. In *The reversible world: Symbolic inversion in art and society*, edited by B. A. Babcock. Ithaca, N. Y.: Cornell University Press, 1978.

Bamberger, B. J. Introduction. In *Reform Judaism: Essays by Hebrew Union College alumni.* Cincinnati: Hebrew Union College Press, 1949.

Becker, H. Sacred and secular societies: Considered with reference to folk-state and similar classifications. *Social Forces* 28 (1950): 361–76.

Bell, D. Reflections on Jewish identity. In *The ghetto and beyond: Essays on Jewish life in America*, edited by P. I. Rose. New York: Random House, 1969.

Bellah, R. N. *Beyond belief: Essays on religion in a post-traditional world.* New York: Harper & Row, 1970.

_____ , ed. *Religion and progress in modern Asia.* New York: Free Press, 1965.

_____ , and Sullivan, W. M. Democratic culture or authoritarian capitalism? *Society* Sept./Oct. 1981: 41–50.

_____ ; Madsen, R.; Sullivan, W. M.; Swidler, A.; and Tipton, S. M. *Habits of the heart: Individualism and commitment in American life.* Berkeley: University of California Press, 1985.

Berger, P. L. *The sacred canopy: Elements of sociological theory of religion.* Garden City, N. Y.: Anchor Books, 1969.

_____ . *A rumor of angels: Modern society and the rediscovery of the supernatural.* Garden City, N. Y.: Anchor Books, 1970.

_____ . *The heretical imperative: Contemporary possibilities of religious affirmation.* Garden City, N. Y.: Doubleday & Co., 1979.

_____ , and Luckmann, T. *The social construction of reality: A treatise in the sociology of knowledge*. Garden City, N. Y.: Anchor Books, 1967.

_____ ; Berger, B.; and Kellner, H. *The homeless mind: Modernization and consciousness*. New York: Vintage Press, 1974.

Bernard, J. *The sociology of community*. Greenview, Ill.: Scott, Foresman & Co., 1973.

Black, C. E. *The dynamics of modernization: A study in comparative history*. New York: Harper & Row, 1966.

Blau, J. L. *Modern varieties of Judaism*. New York: Columbia University Press, 1966.

_____ . *Judaism in America: From curiosity to third faith*. Chicago: University of Chicago Press, 1976.

Bluhm, W. T. *Ideologies and attitudes: Modern political culture*. Englewood Cliffs, N.J.: Prentice-Hall, 1974.

Borowitz, E. B. *The mask Jews wear: The self-deception of American Jewry*. New York: Simon & Schuster, 1973.

_____ . *Reform Judaism today: What we believe* Book 2. New York: Behrman House, 1977.

Brown, R. D. Two Baltic families who came to America: The Jacobsons and the Kruskals, 1870–1970. *American Jewish Archives* 24 (April 1972): 39–93.

Bruner, J. S. *On knowing: Essays for the left hand*. New York: Atheneum, 1965.

Buber, M. *Paths in utopia*. Translated by R. F. C. Hull. New York: Macmillan Co., 1950.

Cahan, A. *The rise of David Levinsky*. New York: Harper & Brothers, 1960.

Carlin, J. E., and Mendlovitz, S. H. The American rabbi: A religious specialist responds to loss of authority. In *Understanding American Judaism: Toward the description of a modern religion*, Vol. 1, edited by J. Neusner. New York: Ktav Publishing House, 1975.

Cassirer, E. *An essay on man: An introduction to a philosophy of human culture*. New Haven: Yale University Press, 1944.

_____ . *The philosophy of the Enlightenment*. Translated by F. C. A. Koelln and J. P. Pettegrove. Princeton, N. J.: Princeton University Press, 1951.

Colaizzi, P. F. Psychological research as the phenomenologist views it. In *Existential phenomenological alternatives to psychology*, edited by R. Valley and M. King. New York: Oxford University Press, 1978.

Cuddihy, J. M. *The ordeal of civility: Freud, Marx, Lévi-Strauss, and the Jewish struggle with modernity.* New York: Dell Publishing Co., 1974.

_____ . *No offense: Civil religion and Protestant taste.* New York: Seabury Press, 1978.

Daily prayer book: Ha-Siddur Ha-Shalem. Translated by P. Birnbaum. New York: Hebrew Publishing Co., 1949.

Davis, M. Jewish religious life and institutions in America (a historical study). In *The Jews: Their religion and culture* 4th ed., edited by L. Finkelstein. New York: Schocken Books, 1971.

Dawidowicz, L. S. Introduction: The world of East European Jewry. In *The golden tradition: Jewish life and thought in Eastern Europe,* edited by L. S. Dawidowicz. Boston: Beacon Press, 1967.

Delattre, R. A. Ritual resourcefulness and cultural pluralism. *Soundings* 61 (1978): 281–301.

Dolgin, J. L. *Jewish identity and the JDL.* Princeton, N. J.: Princeton University Press, 1977.

Douglas, J. D. Deviance and respectability: The social construction of moral meanings. In *Deviance and respectability: The social construction of moral meanings,* edited by J. D. Douglas. New York: Basic Books, 1970.

Douglas, M. *Natural symbols: Explorations in cosmology.* New York: Vintage Books, 1973.

Ducey, M. H. *Sunday morning: Aspects of urban ritual.* New York: Free Press, 1977.

Durkheim, E. *The division of labor in society.* Translated by G. Simpson. New York: Free Press, 1964.

_____ . *The elementary forms of the religious life.* Translated by J. W. Swain. New York: Free Press, 1965.

_____ . *Suicide: A study in sociology.* Edited by G. Simpson and translated by J. A. Spaulding and G. Simpson. New York: Free Press, 1966.

Eisenstadt, S. N. *Tradition, change, and modernity.* New York: John Wiley & Sons, 1973.

Elazar, D. J., and Monson, R. G. The synagogue havurah: An experiment in restoring adult fellowship to the Jewish community. *Jewish Journal of Sociology* 21 (June 1979): 67–80.

Eliade, M. *The sacred and the profane: The nature of religion.* Translated by W. R. Trask. New York: Harcourt, Brace & World, 1959.

Erikson, K. T. *Wayward Puritans: A study in the sociology of deviance*. New York: John Wiley & Sons, 1966.

Fein, L. J.; Chin, R.; Dauber, J.; Reisman, B.; and Spiro, H. *Reform is a verb: Notes on Reform and reforming Jews*. New York: Union of American Hebrew Congregations, 1972.

Feingold, H. L. *Zion in America: The Jewish experience from colonial times to the present*. New York: Hippocrene Books, 1974.

Feldman, A. J. The changing functions of the synagogue and the rabbi. In *Understanding American Judaism: Toward the description of a modern religion*, Vol. 1, edited by J. Neusner. New York: Ktav Publishing House, 1975.

Feuer, L. S. *Ideology and the ideologists*. New York: Harper & Row, 1975.

Fishman, E. M. "Reform: The popularization and politicization of Judaism" (Ph.D. diss., Duke University, 1974). University Microfilms International, 1977, No. 75-2375.

Freund, J. *The sociology of Max Weber*. Translated by M. Ilford. New York: Vintage Books, 1969.

Friedrich, C. J. *Tradition and authority*. London: Pall Mall Press, 1972.

Furman, F. K. Field notes (Unpublished document, 1978).

Gates of the house: The new Union home prayerbook. New York: Central Conference of American Rabbis, 1977.

Gates of prayer: The new Union prayerbook. New York: Central Conference of American Rabbis, 1975.

Geertz, C. *The interpretation of cultures: Selected essays*. New York: Basic Books, 1973.

Glazer, N. *American Judaism*. 2d ed. Chicago: University of Chicago Press, 1972.

Goffman, E. *The presentation of self in everyday life*. Garden City, N. Y.: Anchor Books, 1959.

_____. *Interaction ritual: Essays on face-to-face behavior*. Garden City, N. Y.: Anchor Books, 1967.

Goldscheider, C., and Zuckerman, A. S. *The transformation of the Jews*. Chicago: University of Chicago Press, 1984.

Goldstein, D. S. Open forum: Judaism needs "reforming." *The Jewish Spectator* 39 (Winter 1974): 75-76.

Greeley, A. *Unsecular man: The persistence of religion*. New York: Dell Publishing Co., 1972.

Gusfield, J. R. Tradition and modernity: Misplaced polarities in the study of social change. *American Journal of Sociology* 72 (1967): 351–62.

Heilman, S. C. *Synagogue life: A study in symbolic interaction*. Chicago: University of Chicago Press, 1973.

_____ . Jewish sociologist: Native-as-stranger. *The American Sociologist* 15 (1980): 100–8.

_____ . *The people of the book: Drama, fellowship, and religion*. Chicago: University of Chicago Press, 1983.

Herberg, W. *Protestant, Catholic, Jew: An essay in American religious sociology*. Garden City, N. Y.: Anchor Books, 1960.

Herman, S. N. *Israelis and Jews: The continuity of an identity*. New York: Random House, 1970.

_____ . *Jewish identity: A social psychological perspective*. Beverly Hills, Calif.: Sage Publications, 1977.

Hertzberg, A. The American Jew and his religion. In *American Judaism: Toward the description of a modern religion* Vol. 1, edited by J. Neusner. New York: Ktav Publishing House, 1975.

Heschel, A. J. *The earth is the Lord's: The inner world of the Jew in East Europe*. New York: Harper & Row, 1966. Originally published by Henry Schuman, 1950.

Himmelfarb, H. S. Research on American Jewish identity and identification: Progress, pitfalls, and prospects. In *Understanding American Jewry*, edited by M. Sklare. Center for Modern Jewish Studies, Brandeis University. New Brunswick, N. J.: Transaction Books, 1982.

Himmelfarb, M. *The Jews of modernity*. New York: Basic Books, 1973.

Hoffman, L. A. Creative liturgy. *The Jewish Spectator* 40 (Winter 1975): 42–50.

_____ , The liturgical message. In *Gates of understanding: A companion volume to Shaarei Tefillah, Gates of prayer*, edited by L. A. Hoffman. New York: Union of American Hebrew Congregations, 1977.

Howe, I. *World of our fathers*. New York: Harcourt Brace Jovanovich, 1976.

_____ , and Greenberg, E. Introduction. In *A treasury of Yiddish stories*, edited by I. Howe and E. Greenberg. New York: Schocken Books, 1973.

Huntington, S. P. The change to change: Modernization, development, and politics. *Comparative Politics* 3(1971): 283–322.

Inkeles, A., and Smith, D. H. *Becoming modern: Individual change in six developing countries.* Cambridge, Mass.: Harvard University Press, 1974.

Jacob, W. Prophetic Judaism: The history of a term. *Journal of Reform Judaism* 26 (Spring 1979): 33–46.

Jick, L. A. *The Americanization of the synagogue, 1820–1870.* Hanover, New Hampshire: University Press of New England for Brandeis University Press, 1976.

Kanter, R. M. *Commitment and community: Communes and utopias in sociological perspective.* Cambridge, Mass.: Harvard University Press, 1972.

Karff, S. E. *Agada: The language of Jewish faith.* Cincinnati: Hebrew Union College Press, 1979.

Katz, J. *Tradition and crisis: Jewish society at the end of the Middle Ages.* New York: Free Press of Glencoe, 1961.

———. *Exclusiveness and tolerance: Studies in Jewish-Gentile relations in medieval and modern times.* New York: Schocken Books, 1962.

Kelley, D. M. *Why conservative churches are growing: A study in sociology of religion.* New York: Harper & Row, 1972.

Kerrine, T. M., and Neuhaus, R. J. Mediating structures: A paradigm for democratic pluralism. *Annals of the American Academy of Political and Social Science* 446 (Nov. 1979): 10–18.

Klapp, O. E. *Collective search for identity.* New York: Holt, Rinehart & Winston, 1969.

Knobel, P. S., ed. *Gates of the seasons: A guide to the Jewish year.* New York: Central Conference of American Rabbis, 1983.

Kokosalakis, N. *Ethnic identity and religion: Tradition and change in Liverpool Jewry.* Washington, D. C.: University Press of America, 1982.

Kravitz, L. The Siddur. *Central Conference of American Rabbis Journal.* A special issue on worship and liturgy. n.d., 5–9.

Kroeber, A. L. *Style and civilizations.* Ithaca, N. Y.: Cornell University Press, 1957.

Lasch, C. *The culture of narcissism: American life in an age of diminishing expectations.* New York: W. W. Norton & Co., 1978.

Leach, E. R. Ritual. In *International encyclopedia of the social sciences*, edited by D. L. Sills. 13 (1968): 520–26.

Lelyveld, A. J. Reform Judaism: An insider's evaluation. *Judaism* 89 (Winter 1974): 30–38.

Liebman, C. S. *The ambivalent American Jew: Politics, religion, and family in American Jewish life*. Philadelphia: Jewish Publication Society of America, 1973.

Lifton, R. J. *Boundaries: Psychological man in revolution*. New York: Vintage Books, 1970.

Lofland, J. *Analyzing social settings: A guide to qualitative observation and analysis*. Belmont, Calif.: Wadsworth Publishing Co., 1971.

Luckmann, T. *The invisible religion: The problem of religion in modern society*. New York: Macmillan Co., 1967.

Mannheim, K. *Ideology and utopia: An introduction to the sociology of knowledge*. Translated by L. Wirth and E. Shils. New York: Harcourt, Brace & World, 1936.

Maslin, S. J., ed. *Gates of Mitzvah: A guide to the Jewish life cycle*. New York: Central Conference of American Rabbis, 1979.

Mendelssohn, M. *Jerusalem and other Jewish writings*. Edited by A. Jospe. New York: Schocken Books, 1969.

Meyer, M. A. *The origins of the modern Jew: Jewish identity and European culture in Germany, 1749–1824*. Detroit: Wayne State University Press, 1967.

Mihaly, E. Jewish prayer and synagogue architecture. *Judaism* 7 (Fall 1958): 309–19.

Mirsky, N. B. *Unorthodox Judaism*. Columbus, Ohio: Ohio State University Press, 1978.

Mol, H. J. *Identity and the sacred: A sketch for a new social-scientific theory of religion*. New York: Free Press, 1976.

_____ . The identity model of religion: How it compares with nine other theories of religion and how it might apply to Japan. *Japanese Journal of Religious Studies* 6 (March-June 1979): 11–38.

Moore, S. F., & Myerhoff, B. G. Introduction: Secular ritual: Forms and meanings. In *Secular ritual*, edited by S. F. Moore and B. G. Myerhoff. Assen, The Netherlands: Van Gorcum, 1977.

Neusner, J. *Fellowship in Judaism*. London: Valentine, Mitchell & Co., 1963.

———. *Judaism in a secular age: Essays on fellowship, community and freedom*. New York: Ktav Publishing House, 1970.

———, ed. *Contemporary Judaic fellowship in theory and in practice*. New York: Ktav Publishing House, 1972.

———, ed. *Understanding American Judaism: Toward the description of a modern religion*, 2 Vols. New York: Ktav Publishing House, 1975.

———. *"Being Jewish" and studying about Judaism*. Address and response at the inauguration of the Jay and Leslie Cohen chair of Judaic Studies. Atlanta, Ga.: Emory University Press, 1977.

———. *American Judaism: Adventure in modernity, an anthological essay*. New York: Ktav Publishing House, 1978.

Niebuhr, H. R. *Radical monotheism and Western culture*. New York: Harper & Row, 1960.

———. *The responsible self: An essay in Christian moral philosophy*. New York: Harper & Row, 1963.

Niebuhr, R. *The self and the dramas of history*. New York: Charles Scribner's Sons, 1955.

Nisbet, R. A. *The quest for community: A study in the ethics of order and freedom. New York: Oxford University Press, 1953*.

———. *Twilight of authority*. New York: Oxford University Press, 1975.

Novak, M. *The rise of the unmeltable ethnics: Politics and culture in the seventies*. New York: Macmillan Co., 1972.

———. *The social world of individuals. Hastings Center Studies* 2 (Sept. 1974): 37–44.

O'Dea, T. F. *Sociology and the study of religion: Theory, research, interpretation*. New York: Basic Books, 1970.

Olan, L. A. Rethinking the liberal faith. In *Reform Judaism: Essays by Hebrew Union College alumni*. Cincinnati: Hebrew Union College Press, 1949.

Otto R. *The idea of the holy: An inquiry into the non-rational factor in the idea of the divine and its relation to the rational*. Translated by J. W. Harvey. New York: Oxford University Press, 1958.

Parsons, T. *The social system*. London: Tavistock Publications, 1952.

_____ . *Sociological theory and modern society*. New York: Free Press, 1967.

_____ . *The evolution of societies*. Edited by J. Toby. Englewood Cliffs, N. J.: Prentice-Hall, 1977.

Patai, R. *The Jewish mind*. New York: Charles Scribner's Sons, 1977.

Petuchowski, J. J. *Understanding Jewish prayer*. New York: Ktav Publishing House, 1972.

Philipson, D. *The Reform movement in Judaism*. New and rev. ed. New York: Macmillan Co., 1931.

Plaut, W. G. *The growth of Reform Judaism: American and European sources until 1948*. New York: World Union for Progressive Judaism, 1965.

Plumb, J. H. *The death of the past*. Boston: Houghton Mifflin Co., 1970.

Polish, D. The new Reform and authority. *Judaism* 23 (Winter 1974): 8–22.

Redfield, R. The folk society. *The American Journal of Sociology*, 52 (1947): 293–308.

Reform Judaism, a centenary perspective. *Central Conference of American Rabbis Journal*, 24 (Spring 1977): 7–11.

Reisman, B. *The chavurah: A contemporary Jewish experience*. New York: Union of American Hebrew Congregations, 1977.

Rieff, P. *The triumph of the therapeutic: Uses of faith after Freud*. New York: Harper & Row, 1968.

_____ . Introduction: The impossible culture: Wilde as a modern prophet. In *The soul of man under socialism*, by O. Wilde. New York: Harper & Row, 1970.

Roskies, D. K., and Roskies, D. G. *The shtetl book*. New York: Ktav Publishing House, 1975.

Rotenstreich, N. *Tradition and reality: The impact of history on modern Jewish thought*. New York: Random House, 1972.

Rudolph, L. I., and Rudolph, S. H. *The modernity of tradition: Political development in India*. Chicago: University of Chicago Press, 1967.

Rutman, H. S. Ritual, uniformity, and Reform Judaism. *Central Conference of American Rabbis Journal* 24 (Winter 1977): 89–91.

Schapiro, M. Style. In *Anthropology today: An encyclopedic inventory*. Prepared under the chairmanship of A. L. Kroeber. Chicago: University of Chicago Press, 1953.

Schindler, A. M. Making demands on ourselves. *Reform Judaism* 12 (Spring 1984): 26.

Schutz, A. *Collected papers, Vol. 1.* Edited by M. Natanson. The Hague: Martinus Nijhoff, 1971.

Sellers, J. *Warming fires: The quest for community in America.* New York: Seabury Press, 1975.

Sennet, R. *The fall of public man.* New York: Vintage Books, 1978.

A Shabbat manual. Published for the Central Conference of American Rabbis. New York: Ktav Publishing House, 1972.

Shulman, A. *The old country.* New York: Charles Scribner's Sons, 1974.

Sjoberg, G. Community. In *A dictionary of the social sciences.* New York: Free Press of Glencoe, 1964.

Sklare, M., ed. *The Jews: Social patterns of an American group.* Glencoe, Ill.: Free Press, 1958.

_____. *Conservative Judaism: An American religious movement.* New York: Schocken Books, 1972.

_____, ed. *The Jew in American society.* New York: Behrman House, 1974a.

_____, ed. *The Jewish community in America.* New York: Behrman House, 1974b.

_____, ed. *Understanding American Jewry.* Center for Modern Jewish Studies, Brandeis University. New Brunswick, N. J.: Transaction Books, 1982.

_____, ed. *American Jews: A reader.* New York: Behrman House, 1983.

_____, and Greenblum, J. *Jewish identity on the suburban frontier: A study of group survival in the open society.* New York: Basic Books, 1967.

Slater, P. E. *The pursuit of loneliness: American culture at the breaking point.* Boston: Beacon Press, 1970.

Steinberg, M. *Basic Judaism.* New York: Harcourt, Brace & World, 1947.

Strauss, A. L. *Mirrors and masks: The search for identity.* Glencoe, Ill.: Free Press, 1959.

Sullivan, H. P. Ritual: Attending to the world. *Anglican Theological Review* 15 (June 1975): 9–43.

Tillich, P. *The courage to be.* New Haven: Yale University Press, 1952.

_____. *Dynamics of faith.* New York: Harper Torchbooks, 1958.

Tönnies, F. *Community and society*. Edited and translated by C. Loomis. New York: Harper Torchbooks, 1963.

Transactions of the Parisian Sanhedrin or acts of the assembly of Israelitish deputies of France and Italy. Translated by F. D. Kirwan and collected by D. Tama. In "Readings in modern Jewish history," edited by E. Rivkin. Unpublished manuscript, Hebrew Union College-Jewish Institute of Religion, 1956.

Trilling, L. *Sincerity and authenticity*. Cambridge, Mass.: Harvard University Press, 1972.

Turner, V. *The forest of symbols: Aspects of Ndembu ritual*. Ithaca, N. Y.: Cornell University Press, 1967.

_____ . *The ritual process: Structure and anti-structure*. Chicago: Aldine Publishing Co., 1969.

Underhill, E. *Worship*. New York: Harper Torchbooks, 1957.

The Union prayerbook for Jewish worship. Newly revised edition. New York: Central Conference of American Rabbis, 1956.

Wach, J. *Sociology of religion*. Chicago: University of Chicago Press, 1944.

Weber, M. *From Max Weber: Essays in sociology*. Edited and translated by H. H. Gerth and C. Wright Mills. New York: Oxford University Press, 1972a.

_____ . Traditional authority. In *Readings on premodern societies*, edited by V. Lidz and T. Parsons. Englewood Cliffs, N. J.: Prentice-Hall, 1972b.

Weisberg, H. Ideologies of American Jews. In *The American Jew: A reappraisal*, edited by O. I. Janowsky. Philadelphia: Jewish Publication Society of America, 1964.

Wilson, M. Nyakyusa ritual and symbolism. *American Anthropologist* 56 (April 1954): 228–41.

Yerushalmi, Y. H. *Zakhor: Jewish history and Jewish memory*. Seattle: University of Washington Press, 1982.

Zborowski, M., and Herzog, E. *Life is with people: The culture of the shtetl*. New York: Schocken Books, 1962.

Index